Lifeskills For Adult Children

Janet G. Woititz, Ed.D.
and Alan Garner, M.A.

Health Communications, Inc.
Deerfield Beach, Florida

Library of Congress Cataloging-in-Publication Data

Woititz, Janet Geringer.
    Lifeskills for adult children / by Janet G. Woititz and Alan
Garner.
        p.   cm.
    ISBN 1-55874-070-8
    1. Life skills guides.   2. Adult children of alcoholics — Life
skills guides.   3. Adult children of narcotic addicts — Life
skills guides.   I. Garner, Alan, 1950- . II. Title.
HQ2037.W65 1990   89-28941
362.29'13—dc20   CIP

©1990 Janet G. Woititz and Alan Garner
ISBN 1-55874-070-8

Publisher: Health Communications, Inc.
                3201 S.W. 15th Street
                Deerfield Beach, Florida 33442

Cover design by Vicki Sarasohn

Acknowledgments

I would like to thank
    Linda Cooley
    Robert Henry
    Allen Lukach
    Marc Masino
    Miriam McCoy
    Marguerite Reget
    Barbara Schaeffer
    Ann Stuart
    and
    Roseanna Zoubeck
for their input.

— JGW

To Cindy and Erick for their love and support.

To Rick Potter and his ACoA groups at Safe Harbor in Costa Mesa, California, for their wonderful help and inspiration.

— AG

Contents

v

Introduction

In a family where the first priority is to help the children grow up into mature, happy individuals, the adults of the family teach the younger members the skills they need in order to "do life." Unfortunately all over the world there are adult children who, through no fault of their own, do not have the knowledge they need to live happy, productive lives. Many are lonely and depressed much of the time, have few close friends and no real intimacy. Even if they are married or living with someone, chances are their unions are tumultuous and unsatisfying. We call these people "adult children" because although they are old enough in years to be called adults, they are young enough emotionally to be called children. Their growing has been disrupted because they come from profoundly troubled families.

Many factors can be present to cause a family to be troubled, but among the most common is chemical dependency. Whether it's alcohol or drugs that are making it impossible for the family to function normally, or some other disruption is present, the result is that children of these families grow up without learning some important skills.

If you identify with these adult children, you probably believe that there is something very wrong with you, that there is something missing inside you that other folks have. Not true. There is nothing wrong with you, but there *is* something missing. What is missing is the knowledge of certain specific skills for getting along well with others that most people pick up from their parents.

We wrote *Lifeskills For Adult Children* to teach you these skills. These are the skills you never learned, the skills your parents couldn't teach you, the skills you need to make your life work. Among the skills we will teach you are those for meeting people and making friends, for getting in touch with your feelings and expressing them, for setting up boundaries and defending them, and for working out your problems with others.

Ask yourself if you are having difficulty with any of these skills.

- Starting conversations
- Interesting others in what you have to say
- Expressing emotions
- Asking for what you want
- Giving others what they want
- Solving problems
- Asking others to treat you differently
- Handling criticism
- Saying "No"
- Ending visits, conversations, or relationships.

If you are, this book is for you.

The skills you will learn in this book may be likened to tools. Imagine trying to make pancakes with a hammer or to sweep the floor with a spoon. You could try and try, but you just wouldn't do a very good job. Given the right tools, however, you could make those pancakes and sweep that floor quickly and with very little effort. The same is true for the tools, the skills, you will learn in this book. When you practice using them, you will be amazed at how much better you will be at meeting people and getting along with them. You will be amazed at how much more warmth and love you will bring into your life.

We wish you lots of warmth and lots of love.

— Janet Woititz and Alan Garner

1

Making Contact With Others

I feel like I'm staring at a banquet. All around are
people I'd like to meet, but I never seem to make
contact. The distance between us, it may be just a
few feet, but it feels like a million miles. Everyone
else looks so comfortable and seems to have such an
easy time making friends. If only I knew just the
right thing to say.

— *Terri*

Adult children cringe at the idea of having to make
small talk. Growing up in a dysfunctional family means
that social skills were not adequately developed. Few people really enjoy small talk, but it is a necessary part of the
socialization process.

If you only have started to connect with others since
you've been in recovery, you are learning to relate on the
level of personal problems and pain. That is fine for identifying within the program and appropriate for a support
group, but, the truth is, there is life beyond the programs.

1

In the larger culture, and even with program people outside of meetings, personal problems and pain are best shared with people as intimacy grows. Getting to that level is a part of a process that begins with small talk and evolves from there. Small talk is the most nonthreatening way that people can begin to know each other. People respond as much to tone and energy as to content. Rushing into personal things creates a sense of intimacy before it really exists. And, believe it or not, talking trivia can be fun.

Making contact with others will be easier when you know a few simple truths and develop some skills. The first truth is that most people also feel uncomfortable when they are getting conversations going. They only *look* at ease, just as you probably do to them. Second, most people would like to have more friends in their lives, just as you would. Third, most people are pleased when someone approaches them, as it takes the pressure off them. This chapter will teach you skills that will help you do better in starting conversations, keeping your conversations going, and talking about yourself.

Starting Conversations

There is no need for you, like Terri, to search for "just the right thing to say." The truth is that dull, ordinary openers can work even better than clever openers. The main thing is to say *something*. When you say something, you've made contact, you've opened up the possibility of establishing a relationship, of making a friend. If others are interested, they will respond, and you can apply the skills in this book to use what they say to get a conversation going. There are basically three subjects you can talk about when you start a conversation: yourself, the other person, and the situation.

Talking about the other person or the situation you are both in is far more likely to get the other person involved than only talking about yourself. Why? Because others are much more interested in themselves and what they're doing than they are in you, especially when they don't even know you. When you look at the following openers, you'll see that those on the right, those that talk about the other person or the situation, are far more likely to get conversations going. The best idea is to make the "I" statement first to show your own willingness to share and so as not to appear intrusive.

BEGIN	CONTINUE
I'm looking forward to this movie.	What have you heard about it?
I'm late for work.	Why do you think the bus is late?
I'm a friend of the host.	How did you happen to get invited to this party?

There are basically three things you can say when you start a conversation: You can ask a question, voice an opinion, or state a fact.

To get others to want to join you in conversation, you have to interest and involve them. *Asking questions* is far more likely to do this than relating only your own opinions or stating facts. For example, consider how much more likely the questions on the right are to generate interest than the opinions or facts on the left:

BEGIN	CONTINUE
There are a lot of people here.	Why do you suppose so many people came to this speech?
This washing machine is hard to work.	Can you show me how to work it?
That book looks interesting.	What's it about?

Most people are *reactive* when it comes to starting conversations. Like Terri, they see people they'd like to meet, people they'd like to make friends with, yet they don't do anything about it. People who succeed socially are typically *proactive*. They don't sit around waiting for others to come up to them; *they* speak up, *they* make things happen. If you want to succeed at friendmaking — or at practically anything else — you need to be proactive.

EXERCISE: Write down the 10 best things that have ever happened to you. Next, write down whether you or others were responsible for making each of those things happen. Chances are, you will find that most or all of the highlights of your life happened only because *you* took action and were proactive.

Marika: I was stunned when I did this exercise. Here I've been more or less waiting for things to happen in my life, and it turns out that . . . my going to Europe, my trip to Maui, my meeting my husband, my friendship with Leslie, my job — virtually everything that's been positive and wonderful in my life has happened because of me!

Being proactive in starting conversations is often difficult, especially for women who have been taught they *"should"* be passive. Often these women take this *should* to an extreme and not only don't say anything to people they'd like to meet, but also don't smile, look at others, or give any other indication of interest. Following this rule deprives them of any realistic likelihood of making contact. But it also provides them with an excuse: They don't have to blame themselves for not getting what they want. They can blame the *should*.

If you have been following this *should* (or any other *should*, for that matter), ask yourself: "Who made up this rule?" Chances are you will find that your mother, a teacher, or some other authority figure in your early childhood told you to follow this rule. Tell yourself that it was just their opinion. It was just something they made up — or more likely learned from *their* parents. It isn't carved in stone anywhere. It isn't any great piece of wisdom. And there's no reason for you to go on obeying it. Tell yourself you're an adult now and you can make up your own mind. Then go ahead and speak up.

Many people have difficulty starting conversations because they tell themselves that it would be "awful," "horrible," and "humiliating" if the others weren't interested. When you find yourself thinking thoughts like that, ask yourself: "What, realistically, is the worst thing that might happen if I speak up?" Chances are, the worst thing others might do is excuse themselves or walk away. Tell yourself: "If that happened, it would not be terrible. It would just be unfortunate. I don't want it to happen, but I'd live. In fact, I'd be no worse off. I didn't have that person's attention before and I still wouldn't." In addition, remind yourself that you are better off simply for practicing your new skills, regardless of the response. Each time you practice, you get better and better. Then ask yourself: "What's the best thing that might happen?" Looking at it this way, you'll be surprised how vastly more you have to gain than lose by speaking up.

> *Elise:* I wanted to meet this fellow who lived in another building at my complex. Smiling and saying hello didn't work, so I asked myself, "What's the worst that could happen if I start a conversation?" The worst was that he'd say he had to go or that he was busy. Then I asked, "What's the best?" The best was that we'd like each other, get married, and have a lifetime of kisses and cuddles and happy times. Looking at it that way, there was only one smart choice — and I did it!

EXERCISE: The next time you find yourself "awfulizing," carry your thoughts to an extreme. For example, if you're thinking about starting a conversation with someone and are worried about being rejected, imagine that person not only rejecting you but also loudly telling everyone in the vicinity that you tried to be friendly. Imagine that person calling up your boss — and getting you fired! Imagine that person calling up your parents or your children — and getting you rejected for the "awful" thing you have done. Carrying your thoughts to an extreme can help you look at your worst fears and see how absurd most of them are most of the time.

Homework: Set goals for yourself for starting conversations over the next week. Start wherever you feel comfortable. If you're not used to starting conversations, perhaps a goal of smiling at someone might be right for you. Perhaps your goal will be to start a conversation once a day with people you already know. Here are some sample goals you can choose from, combine, or modify for the next week.

- Smile at someone once a day for a week. Do not attempt to get a conversation going.
- Smile at two people a day for a week. Do not attempt to get a conversation going.
- Smile at three people a day for a week. Do not attempt to get a conversation going.

Write out your goal for the week, whatever it is, and post it somewhere you will see it and be reminded of it frequently. Many people post it on their bathroom mirror, on their "To Do" list, or in their datebook. After you have achieved your goal for the day, make a note of it, perhaps with a check mark next to the date. Reward yourself daily when you fulfill your goal, both with your congratulations and with something you would not ordinarily get — perhaps a nice warm bubble bath or a 30-minute walk. Small or large, the only requirement is that your reward be something you want.

Your goal is achieved when you do what you set out to do, regardless of whether the other person responds positively. If you don't achieve a goal one day, don't put yourself down. Just get back on track and pick up where you left off the next day. If you are having a hard time remembering to keep your goals, decide to do it each day *before* you do something else — say, like taking your lunch break.

Once you have completed your first week, build on that success each of the following weeks by advancing one more step on the list. You will grow more self-confident and skillful, and your social life will flower as you continue to do this homework. Eventually, you will come to the end of the list, and your goal at that point might be to maintain your level as long as it seems beneficial to you.

Each and every day, no matter which goal you are working on, spend five minutes a day vividly picturing yourself in your mind's eye smiling confidently as you complete that goal. Picture those you are speaking with distinctly, what they look like, what they're wearing. Imagine them returning your smile and responding positively. Such covert rehearsals can contribute greatly to success. Basketball, football, hockey players, public speakers — successful people from all walks of life — can attest to the tremendous value of imagining success over and over in your mind before you go for the real thing. What you see in your mind can be what you get.

Keeping Your Conversations Going

The most important skills you can use to keep your conversations going are *asking questions* and *picking up on conversational cues.*

Asking Questions

Lorraine: I started a conversation with my new neighbor and decided, after a while, that it might be interesting to learn more about her. "So," I said, "What do you do?"

"I'm a teacher," she replied.

"What do you teach?" I asked.

"French," she replied.

"In junior high, high school, or college?" I asked.

"Junior high school," she replied.

"Do you like it?" I asked.

"Yes," she replied.

On and on I went. I tried and tried, but the conversation never really got going. After a while, I started feeling like a police officer grilling a suspect. Finally I said, "Nice meeting you," and left.

When your questions draw only one or two word answers, it may not be that others aren't interested in talking to you. The problem may simply be that you are asking the wrong type of questions.

Closed Questions

Closed questions ask for specific information — and that's usually all they get. Closed questions commonly begin with any form of "Do" or "Are," as well as with "Who," "When," "Where," and sometimes "What." For example:

"Do you plan to stop at the bookstore?"

"Are you interested in stocks and bonds?"

"Who are you taking to the party?"

"When is Madge coming back?"

"What movie do you most want to see?"

"Where are you going on your next vacation?"

To encourage others to answer your closed questions, it sometimes helps to model the responses you want:

"My name's Deborah. What's your name?"

"I live in Lexington. Where do you live?"

"My number's 555-8215. What's yours?"

Closed questions can provide you with valuable information that you can follow up on to keep your conversations going. But if you ask too many in a row, you, like Lorraine, will soon start sounding like an interrogator.

Open Questions

Follow up your closed questions with open questions if you really want to get your conversations going. Open questions are those that ask for more than just a one or two word answer. They encourage others to explore their thoughts by asking for explanations and elaborations. Open questions normally begin with "How," "Why," and "Tell me about," and sometimes with "What." For example:

"How did you get involved with Big Sisters?"

"Why did you find it so hard to leave Wall Street?"

"Tell me about the toughest challenge you faced."

"What do you think caused Josh to change his mind?"

To produce more interesting answers, ask for the highlights of others' experiences. Ask, for example, for "the most," "the best," "the hardest," "the most memorable":

"What was the most exciting scene in that movie?"

"Tell me about your greatest golf shot."

"Tell me about the hardest part of the climb."

"What was the highlight of your trip?"

Frequently you will need to start out with a closed question ("What do you do?") before following up with an open question ("Really! How did you get into that field?"). Remember, closed questions are not "bad" or "wrong." They have a very important function to play in conversation. The only time they become a problem is when you ask three or more of them in a row.

Too Open Questions

Beware of making your questions *too* open. Questions like "What's new?" and "Tell me about yourself" ask for so much information, that all they typically elicit are closed answers like "Nothing" or "There isn't much to tell."

Surprisingly enough, the average husband and wife talk to each other just five minutes a day. Often, too open questions are to blame. Suppose, for example, a wife comes home at the end of the day and her husband says to her, "What did you do today, dear?" Now, perhaps during that day she drove to work, got in a traffic jam, filled out lots of forms, tried to make nine sales, had a customer call with a complaint, discussed her commission structure with her boss, and drove back home. Now, how likely is she to answer that question fully and tell her husband *everything* that happened? Not likely at all. It would take an hour or two. So what will she do? She'll probably respond to that too open question with closed answers like, "Oh, the usual."

Many husbands and wives, confronted with such closed answers, often complain and accuse the other person of being unwilling to talk, when all they really need to do is use the right tool, open questions. The husband in our example might have enjoyed far more luck by focusing on just one of his wife's sales and saying, "Tell me about today's toughest customer."

It may have occurred to you that closed questions occasionally do get open answers. For example, you may have sometime asked someone, "Did you have a nice trip?" and found that this did, in fact, inspire the other person to talk on a bit about the trip. While this does happen now and then, more often people respond to closed questions with a one word answer like "Yes." Open questions are the right tools for getting others to open up, and you will find they will work for you better and much more consistently.

You may find it helpful to prepare some questions in advance, when possible. This will make it less likely that you will ever be at a loss for words. Consider Zoe's experience: "The gal who usually sits next to me in my ACoA group is in sales. I'd wanted to speak with her during the break but never had. As I was driving to the meeting, I asked myself, 'What can I ask someone in sales?' I came up with all sorts of questions like, 'How did you get started in sales?' 'Tell me about your toughest sale . . . your easiest sale.' Well, it worked like a charm! The only problem I had was ending the conversation when it came time to go back to group!"

Picking Up On Conversational Cues

During the course of your conversations, others will frequently give you more information than you asked for.

Consider these examples, with the extra information, the conversational cues, in italic type:

> *Joan:* Your Royal Cruise Line T-shirt looks very sporting. Have you been on one of their cruises?
> *Jane:* Yeah, *I went on their Caribbean cruise.*

> *Dave:* How long have you had a computer?
> *Louis:* A year. *My wife insisted I get it.*

> *Cybel:* Aren't you new to this church?
> *Scott:* Yes, *I just got transferred here from Charleston.*

By following up on these conversational cues, you'll let others know that you are interested, and you'll keep your conversations going while steering them in interesting directions. To catch these conversational cues, all you do is make comments or ask questions (preferably open questions) about them. Joan, Dave, and Cybel, for example, might follow up on the examples above in the following ways:

> *Joan:* Really, what was the highlight of your cruise?

> *Dave:* Why did she insist?

> *Cybel:* How come they transferred you here?

In addition to what others say, conversational cues you can pick up on include others' clothes, jewelry, accents, books they are carrying, trophies, photos, and art. You'll be amazed how following up on these cues can open up your conversations. Consider Marsha's example:

> *Marsha:* The boss called me up to his office to welcome me aboard, and I was nervous as can be! *No* idea what to say. As I entered the room to get my greeting, I noticed a couple of golf trophies and I said, "I see you play golf." Not the most brilliant comment ever made, but it got him talking. "What one shot did you make that clinched this one?" I asked, and his face lit up as he described it. On and on he went. Instead of a quick, "Welcome to the company," I got a full hour of his time! Twice now, when he's needed someone to complete a foursome, he's invited me. And he introduces me as a rising young star at the company!

Homework: At least once a day for the next week, practice keeping a conversation going by asking open questions and following up on conversational cues.

Talking About Yourself

Starting conversations, asking questions, and picking up on conversational cues will help you get to know others, but it won't help them get to know you. The people you meet are interested in talking, but they're also interested in listening. Many adult children wonder why their conversations — and their relationships — often don't really get going. Sometimes the reason is that they never spoke up and gave others the chance to get to know them. Look at the strangers driving down the street sometime and ask yourself how much you really care about those people. Sure, you care in the abstract, but chances are that the truth, on an individual level, is "not much." People only really care about those they have gotten to know, those they have gotten involved with. And they will only get involved with you when you speak up and talk about yourself.

People normally reveal themselves at about the same rate. One person says something about herself in the hope that the other person will both want to learn more and will join in the self-disclosure. You can encourage this process by talking about yourself and by responding to what others say with questions and comments. Here is an example of how this can work:

> *Marie:* Hello. Aren't you new to this ACoA group?
> *Cindy:* Yes, I used to come to the Tuesday night group, but it got too large for me.
> *Marie:* I know what you mean. I switched from that group myself. I find it hard to get to know people in larger groups. Say, my name's Marie. What's yours?
> *Karen:* Karen. What sort of work do you do?
> *Marie:* I'm a dietician. How about yourself?
> *Karen:* I'm a speech therapist.
> *Marie:* I work for the city schools. Where do you work?

Karen: I'm with the county. I'm curious, what exactly do you do as a dietician?

When you talk about yourself, the things you say will tend to be interesting when you do three things: *use dual perspective, get specific,* and *share yourself.*

Use Dual Perspective

Have you ever noticed what you were doing differently when you were most successful in interesting others? Chances are that you were thinking not just about what you wanted to say but also about what others were likely to enjoy hearing and discussing. Thinking about both yourself *and* the other person is using dual perspective. Using dual perspective will help you not only in using this skill but in successfully using all the other skills in this book as well.

To use dual perspective, ask yourself: "What is this person likely to be interested in discussing?" If nothing comes to mind, put yourself into the other person's shoes and ask yourself, "What would I want to discuss if I were in her (or his) situation?" Then pick one of those topics that is of interest to you also. Great conversations tend to come from finding topics that both of you are interested in and can discuss. For example, you have just returned from a vacation spent driving along the East Coast. Your conversational partner asks you the too open question, "What did you do on your trip?" You ask yourself, "What is he likely to be interested in discussing?" and you recall that he is a traveling salesman who spends weeks at a time on the road. So you talk about, and you ask him about, topics like your worst and best meal, avoiding tickets, and locating good hotels.

Here is a second example: A friend confides in you that her husband has filed for a divorce. Your first thought is to tell her you're sure he'll change his mind. Using dual perspective, you ask yourself, "What is she likely to be interested in discussing?" Instead of dismissing the problem, you ask her how she's handling it. Then you relate as similar a situation as you can come up with. If you haven't been divorced, you can talk about a painful breakup you've had.

As the conversation proceeds, continue using dual perspective by speaking about and asking questions about topics that interest you, while taking into account the other person's enthusiasms. On what topics do they seem to be moving to the edge of their seats and leaning forward? When are they gesturing a lot, when do their faces seem to come alive? When do their voices sound excited? Chances are those are topics they'd like to pursue further.

Get Specific

General talk tends to be boring. Talk that focuses on specifics, and especially on highlights, tends to be interesting. For example, if someone asks about your trip to the country and you say, "I saw lots of interesting things and met many interesting people," that's boring! It would be more interesting for you, using dual perspective, to focus on *one* of those things you saw, *one* of those people you met: "I ran across a teacher I used to know who left town and moved to the country. He said one particular class had driven him to leave . . ." Getting specific about that man and that class might well be interesting for you and the other person. Also, it might well lead to interesting discussions about topics like giving it all up and moving to the country and the lack of discipline in our schools.

Share Yourself

When you talk about yourself, don't just state facts. Your conversation will be far more interesting when you tell how *you* relate to those facts. Own your statements by using the word "I" when you are talking about yourself. When you fail to use the word "I," people often won't understand who the events happened to. For example: "You wouldn't believe the service! You go off to dinner, and someone cleans up your room while you're gone! If you decide on the buffet, someone's there to take your tray and walk it to your table!" The speaker was talking about her trip, but her use of the word "you" made it seem like it was the listener who had the experience.

Look at how much clearer the message would have been if the speaker had owned her statements by using the word "I": "I couldn't believe the service! I'd go off to dinner, and someone would clean up my room while I was gone! If I decided on the buffet, someone was there to take my tray and walk it to my table!"

Another way you may confuse ownership of statements is by assigning ownership not to "I" or to "you" but to no one. This is easily fixed by simply starting your sentences with an "I." For example:

INSTEAD OF SAYING . . .	SAY . . .
"It was scary."	"I was scared!"
"What a disappointment!"	"I was disappointed."
"That was interesting."	"I found that interesting."

Another way in which you may be camouflaging your ownership of statements is by disguising your opinions, feelings, or desires as questions. Saying, "Haven't you worked enough?" gives only the vaguest hint that what you meant was, "I want some attention." Saying, "Wouldn't you rather stay home?" doesn't make it at all clear that what you meant was, "I want you to stay home." When you express your thoughts by beginning them with the word "I," you won't run into that confusion. For example:

INSTEAD OF SAYING . . .	SAY . . .
"Isn't it getting late?"	"I'm tired and I want to go."
"Isn't 20 miles too far to drive to a restaurant?"	"I want to eat somewhere closer."

| "What do you think about vacationing in Disney World this year?" | "I want to go to Disney World this year." |

Disguising your thoughts not only confuses the situation, it costs you power. When you say, for example, "Shall we go to a movie?" you are far more likely to get turned down ("No, let's stay home") than when you own your own thoughts and say, "I want to go to a movie."

Homework: At least once a day for the next week, practice sharing yourself.

Another way you can share yourself is by expressing your feelings. The entire subject of feelings will be the focus of the next chapter.

2

Expressing Feelings

Alternate Solutions

What would I do to Father if my father did to me
The scary things he did before, when I was only three?
The frightening uncertainties, the mad, malicious laugh
That stole away my childhood and bent my soul in half.

I would chain him to the swing set and leave him in the rain,
I would shine a flashlight in his eyes to brighten up his brain.
I'd tie him in a figure-eight and bounce him down the stairs,
I'd soak his head and one by one I'd pull out all his hairs.

What would I do to Father if he stepped inside my door
And tickled me and teased me like when I was only four?
He taunted me and called me names and blew smoke in my eye,
Then smiled a toothy little smile and told me not to cry.

I would call him names right back and I'd light up a big cigar,
I'd send him off to China in a drafty railroad car,

I'd hang him by his ankles and make faces while he yelled,
I'd cook him up in gelatin and mold him in a gel.

What would I do to Dad if he ever dared contrive
To stomp around like he would do when I was only five?
He lumbered like a monster and he bellowed like a hound,
And made life pretty miserable for everyone around.

I would hire a team of surgeons to dissect his larynx out,
Put tacks in both his shoes so he would hurt to stomp about.
If he acted like a monster, I would put him in a cage,
And pull a velvet curtain down when he was in a rage.

What would I do to Dad, and I wouldn't hesitate
If he acted like he did when I was six and seven and eight?
If he criticized the way I looked or slapped me on the head,
Or otherwise rejected me or filled me full of dread?

I would tell him he was full of shit, and I was not to blame,
For I am good and brave and strong and he is put to shame.
I'd sell him to a circus. What a lovely price they'd pay.
I'd spend the money on a car and slowly drive away.

What would I do to Dad if he tried to make me cower,
Like when I was just nine or ten and didn't know my power,
If he would be a tyrant about everything I did,
Or if he would be annoyed that I was being just a kid.

I would tell him to shut up and then I'd slap him on the face.
I would make him tie my shoe, not the Velcro kind, the lace.
I would sit him down in front of me and deftly box his ear.
And if he kept on yelling, he would simply disappear.

This poem was written by an adult child who is learning to identify and express her emotions. Like her, you may have been deeply hurt when you were little. So intense was your pain that you denied your feelings in order to survive. Now that you're an adult, you may still be denying your feelings. The terror and insecurity of the past are long gone, and it is time to learn how to identify and express your feelings.

Identifying Your Feelings

Be honest about your feelings. If you're typical, you are often not truthful about your feelings. You pretend to be happy when you're not. You pretend to be self-assured when you're afraid. This is easy for you because you grew up in a family where this was the norm. If your father or mother was an alcoholic, you all pretended everything was okay. Dad hadn't passed out on the floor — he was just tired. Mom wasn't suffering from a hangover — she was just sick. You may not only have lied to each other, you may have lied to yourself as well, telling yourself you weren't really seeing what you were seeing, hearing what you were hearing, and feeling what you were feeling.

It may be a long time since you have lived with your parents, but even now, you still continue the pattern. Chances are you lie about lots of things, but most of all, you are not honest about your feelings.

Homework: The first step to take in tackling the problem of lying is to become aware of it. You can do so by keeping a diary for the next week in which you record the times you lie about your feelings.

When you lie, very often it's because you're afraid of being rejected. You think that if people knew you were as you are, they'd abandon you. Most likely, however, your friends *do* know you, and they like and accept you anyway.

While it's true that if you are open, you may be rejected, it's also true that being honest about your feelings is the only path to true acceptance. Suppose, for example, that you do trick someone into accepting and liking and maybe even loving some phony you. What have you got? Nothing. You can't experience any positive feelings they express towards you as your own. It's that false you that's being accepted, liked and loved. By contrast, if you took the chance of expressing your real feelings, you might be able to enjoy real friendship and intimacy. So it doesn't pay to pretend, because when you do so, even when you win, you lose.

Once you become aware that you do lie, resolve to stop it. Just like an alcoholic in AA, you can resolve not to lie — today. Don't worry about stopping for the rest of your life. Just do it one day at a time. Should you find yourself once again lying, don't put yourself down. Just spend some time thinking and writing about what you said and why you lied. The next day, resolve to do better. If, after several days, you still find yourself lying, tell yourself that the next time you lie, you will correct yourself then and there.

> *Kevin:* I couldn't believe it. Rosemarie asked how I'm feeling and I said, "Great!" Then I stopped myself and said, "The truth is, my mother's sick and I'm worried about her." I was concerned that if I sounded depressed, Rosemarie would take off. Instead, she began telling me about how difficult her own mother's illness had been for her. Through our sharing, we've reached a closeness we never had before.

The next step in identifying your feelings is to focus attention on them. If you're typical, your life is loaded with stimuli — television shows, radio shows, the news, music, your family, your job, traffic. These stimuli and more occupy you day and night and make it easy for you to ignore your feelings. To get in touch with your feelings, it helps to remove yourself from that noise and to quiet down. The following exercise will help:

EXERCISE: Find a dark, quiet room where you can relax without being disturbed. Sit back in a comfortable chair or lie down on a couch or bed. Close your eyes. Relax. For the next three minutes, do nothing except feel whatever emotions come to you . . .

When the three minutes are up, focus on your breathing . . . Feel your nostrils as your breath moves in and out through them . . . Feel how your chest rises and falls as you inhale and exhale . . .

Focus on your feet. What are they feeling . . . ? A little itchy perhaps . . . ? Are they warm or cool? Stretch them out and see how they feel . . .

Focus on the rest of your legs. Don't hurry. Take at least one minute to pay attention to your legs and to each of the other parts of your body . . . Then focus on your stomach and chest. Any tension there . . . ? Your back? Take your time and feel whatever there is to feel there . . . Your shoulders . . .? Your neck — are the muscles there a little tight . . . ? Your face? What are your eyeballs feeling . . . ?

Next, focus on what you're feeling . . . Not how you "should" feel but how you *do* feel.

Do this exercise once a day for at least the next week. You'll find yourself becoming more and more connected with your emotions. It may be difficult if you have been out of touch with your feelings for some time. Your emotions may be deeply buried inside you. They may be ever so quiet and hard to detect. Take your time. Be relaxed about it. Do the exercise every day, and let your emotions emerge from hiding little by little.

Name Your Feelings

Once you have got in touch with your feelings, it's time to begin to name them. Naming your emotions will take away some of the uncertainty and mystery and fear that sometimes surround them. When you name your feelings, you are far less likely ever to feel overwhelmed by them.

Feelings can be summarized in a single word. Further, there are only four basic ones: *glad, mad, sad* and *scared.* When you begin to identify your emotions, simply pick out which of the four basic ones you are feeling. If that's not immediately apparent, look to your body for clues. If your fist is closed, your jaw is tight, and your heart is pounding, you are probably mad. If your eyes are turned down a lot, your shoulders are hunched, and you're talking and walking slowly, you're probably sad. If you're just not sure what you feel, guess and see if your guess seems correct.

Identify Shades Of Feeling

Once you have mastered naming the basic feelings, it is time to begin thinking in terms of shades of feeling. There's a wide difference between being "pleased" and "ecstatic," between being "scared" and "petrified." Here is a list of feelings, written in the form you will use them when you say, "I feel _____ ." They may prove helpful to you in identifying shades of feeling.

Sad	Mad	Glad	Scared
ashamed	angry	blissful	afraid
bored	annoyed	calm	anxious
depressed	disgusted	cheerful	concerned
discouraged	distraught	comfortable	confused
embarrassed	frustrated	confident	insecure
guilty	irritated	encouraged	nervous
helpless	jealous	excited	panicky
hurt	offended	fulfilled	shocked
lonely	resentful	happy	tense
regretful		loving	terrified
sickened		overjoyed	uncertain
tired		passionate	
uncomfortable		pleased	
unhappy		relieved	
weary			

Another valuable way of approaching feelings is to identify the *degree* to which you experience a particular emotion. Are you "somewhat" pleased or "very" pleased? Are you "a little" worried or "very" worried? Making these distinctions may be difficult at first. Since you may not be used to registering any emotions at all, even slight emotions may at first be felt intensely. You may find you have a tendency at first to minimize or rationalize your emotions. If you find yourself doing this, pause and let your emotions flow, let your emotions come out as they will. Feel your emotions in any intensity you feel them, knowing that you will be all right.

At the beginning, you may find yourself often registering your emotions as anger when, in fact, you felt another emotion *just before* you felt the anger. Gretchen, for example, was asked by her parents how she was doing on her diet. She felt angry at her mother for asking, but only later did she realize that the first emotion she had felt was embarrassment for obviously having gotten heavier.

Homework: Go to an ACoA meeting. Listen — not for content, but for feelings and for how they are expressed. One thing you'll surely note is how typical your feelings are.

Homework: Over the next week, keep a "Feeling Diary," recording the emotions you feel every two hours during the day. Use your list to identify those emotions. You'll be surprised by the rich variety of emotions you'll be writing down in your diary.

EXERCISE: Find someone with whom you would feel safe discussing personal matters. It may be a neighbor, a teacher, a best friend, a husband or wife, a brother or sister, or perhaps a therapist. Tell that person you're working on better expressing emotions and ask for help and understanding. As a first exercise, get a set of 3 x 5 cards. On each one, write an emotion from your list of feelings. Take turns picking a card and describing a time when you felt the feeling on it.

Expressing Positive Feelings

Once you have got in touch with your feelings and adept at naming them, the next step is to express them, beginning with positive feelings. If you are like most adult children, positive feelings are difficult for you to express. Your parents often criticized you and seldom expressed positive feelings toward you. Given this modeling, it's understandable that you tend to do the same. If you are to become a more positive person, it will take considerable conscious effort, but you *can* do it.

The people you know yearn to hear more positive comments about themselves. Most people are quick to point out the negative while simply ignoring the positive. If you become one of the few — and very likely the only person — in their lives who has anything positive to say, you will be highly valued as a friend. Further, the atmosphere of warmth and acceptance you will bring to their lives will help others to flower and grow.

Become A Compliment Detective

Begin by making a deliberate search for things you like. Become a "compliment detective." Carefully look for things you appreciate about others' *behavior, appearance,* and *possessions.* Carry around a pen and paper and set a daily goal of spotting and writing down ten positives a day. You'll find lots to like when you begin making the effort. Even when you see someone fail, you can still admire their effort.

The first week or two, *don't say anything.* Your goal is simply to observe and write. Review your list now and then in your spare time and dwell on how much you liked some things. When your eyes turn to something they don't like, just pass on over it and look for the positive. Slowly, subtly, you'll find your attitude shifting. You'll be feeling warmer, more positive, more appreciative of others. You'll be seeing that even people you didn't especially like have a lot going for them.

> *Terry:* I had a blind date and I thought, "Well, this will be a good place to start." I looked at him and saw that he wasn't standing up straight, his clothes were polyester, his hair wasn't combed . . . Then I began looking for the positive, and I saw that his tie was gorgeous, he had a cute smile, and a lot of things he said were really very worth hearing.

Deliver Your Compliment

Once you have become good at being a compliment detective, it's time to share some of your feelings with others. The following three-step formula will make it easy: (1) Be specific. (2) Say the person's name. (3) Follow up with a question.

1. *Be specific:* Tell the other person exactly what you like about their behavior, appearance, or possessions:

"I admire the way you ask again and again for the sale."

"You must be working out. I'd say you've lost five pounds."

"I love this leather seat. It feels so rich and comfortable to sink into."

Beware of complimenting the other person as a whole.

"You're terrific."

"You're such a good boy."

"You're so beautiful."

Overly broad compliments such as these tend to have far less impact than do more specific ones. Partly this is because they are usually not believed. No one thinks they are 100 percent terrific, good, or beautiful, and so people tend to silently reject such statements. Also, if your hope is to encourage the other person to repeat a behavior you liked, you are far more likely to accomplish this if you tell them specifically what you liked. Statements like "You're terrific" offer little to go on in deciding how to please you in the future.

2. *Say the person's name.* Dale Carnegie wrote, "A man's name is to him the sweetest and most important sound in the English language." Using a person's name heightens a compliment and makes it seem uniquely suited to that person:

"Mandy, I appreciate your volunteering to wash the car."

"Andrea, that shorter hairstyle will be just right for your new job. It's soft, yet serious."

"Steve, your car really responds when I accelerate."

3. *Follow up with a question:* Many people get embarrassed when they are complimented. As a result, they will often deny your compliments ("You like this old dress?") or downplay them ("Actually, it's just something I threw on."). You can help them receive your compliments by following them up with questions, especially open questions. Then, instead of fishing about for a response, they can simply answer your questions.

Homework: Using the three-step formula, deliver one compliment every day for the next ten days.

Indirect Compliments

You can powerfully signal your appreciation and admiration without delivering a direct compliment. For example:

Linda: My father showed me I was important by taking some time every day to talk with me. He'd drop everything, kneel down to my level, and give me his complete attention as we chatted. I felt wonderful — so special!

Avia: My husband opens my car door first, before his. A small thing, but it lets me know he cares for me and respects me.

Jack: I told a friend I had a cold, and the next day a *big* bottle of vitamins arrived from him! It's a great present. I think nice thoughts about him the first thing in the morning and the last thing at night!

Carol: When I completed Step Six, my step-study leader showed up with a rose for me!

Barbara: I get migraines, and a friend sends me an article now and then on how to prevent them. It lets me know he cares.

Robert: I had told Becky I might want to get into import/ export but wasn't sure what to do. A few weeks later, a ticket arrived. She had paid for me to take "How to Succeed in Import/Export"!

Pay attention, look around, and you'll find lots of opportunities to pay your own indirect compliments.

Homework: Plan and deliver one indirect compliment each day for the next ten days. It can be something as simple as standing aside and letting someone else pass first through a doorway — or it can be much more.

Saying "I Love You"

"I love you" is the positive statement some people in your life most want to hear from you — and seldom if ever do. When you part, you say, "Bye-bye" or "Nice talking to you," when what you really want to say is, "I love you." You close letters with "Sincerely" or "Your friend," or even "Love ya," when what you really want to write is "I love you." You shake hands and maybe even give a hug, but what is left unsaid is "I love you."

People can't read your mind. They don't know how you feel unless you tell them. If you love them, the only way they can be certain is if you say so.

It isn't enough to smile or hint or treat people well or use a stamp that says "LOVE" on it. If you love someone, they want to hear it from you.

Consider this story from a nurse named Jill: "One of the patients at the rest home where I work was in tears. When I asked him what was the matter, he said his son had called and had told him 'I love you' for the first time, just before hanging up. The old man said he called back and, his voice shaking, said, 'I love you too' — and then he hung up also!"

One easy way to start out is to say it in writing. No need to make a big deal out of it — just close your letter with "Love" or "I love you."

Another way to begin is to say it parenthetically, as a student named Jim did: "One day, my folks and I were talking, and they said they were heading out in a storm. 'I love you,' I said, 'and I don't want you to get hurt. So how about if I drive?' As we were driving along in the rain, no one said anything, but my mom had tears in her eyes."

One thing more: People don't just want to hear it once, they want to hear again and again that they are loved.

Don't be like the busy businessman who, when asked by his wife if he loved her, said, "Look, I told you 20 years ago, and if I'd changed my mind, I'd have let you know." Others may have difficulty accepting your positive feelings, but a caring thought is never harmful.

Expressing Negative Feelings

Anger is the most difficult of all emotions for you to express. As a child you saw that your parents' anger often led to violence, and any expression of your own anger often led to punishment. As a result, you learned to deny or hold in your anger, even though you were filled with rage.

Your parents may be long gone, but as an adult child you're still bottling up your anger. You sometimes feel like a time bomb ticking away, waiting to explode with anger. You do burst forth with anger now and then, often in a way totally out of proportion to the situation. You may just be mad about some small thing — but you let others have it for everything. As a practical matter, you see your choice as being between continuing to bottle up your anger and exploding with it. Fortunately, there are alternatives. Consider the following suggestions.

Speak Up About Minor Irritations

Begin by expressing minor irritations. Use the list of feelings when you need help identifying how you feel. Like a safety valve on a pressure cooker, expressing irritations allows you to release annoyances before they build into anger. Also, when you express your dislike of the actions of others, it is far more likely that they will stop than if you just wait and hope.

Pause

When you feel a surge of anger, pause and wait for it to diminish. If you have to, walk away. If you act on the basis of your initial bursts of anger, your responses may be extreme, and you may regret the things you'll do or say.

Blair: I can't tell you how often I've almost hit my young son
— and didn't. He refuses to eat his dinner or he's stalling at
bedtime, and I want to hit him. At those times, I pause and
go get a glass of water. I go to the bathroom. I walk around
the block. Anything. During the pause, my feelings usually
change, and I become relieved I didn't hit him. In fact, I
sometimes end up secretly admiring him for sticking up for
his views about dinner, for putting me off so well at bedtime.

Be Clear And Direct

Let the other person know exactly how you feel. Summarize your feelings in one word:
"I feel *angry* that you're late and didn't call."
"I'm *upset* that you didn't show up."
"I'm *mad* at you for borrowing my car." If you are
indirect ("I wish you hadn't borrowed my car"), people
may not know how strongly you feel. If you not only want
to express your anger, but also want others to change
their behavior, consider using the "When . . . then" formula outlined in Chapter 7.

Own Your Own Feelings

Statements beginning with "You" indicate blame. Saying, "You make me angry" wrongly places responsibility
for how you feel at the feet of others. You are ultimately
responsible for your feelings. Let your language reflect
this reality by beginning your feeling statements with "I":
"I feel angry that you aren't ready."
"I'm furious that you lied to me."
"I'm upset that you criticized me in front of my son."

Write Out Your Anger

Many adult children, like the woman whose poem began this chapter, find relief by expressing their emotions
in writing. You can do it in a journal that only you read, or
you can do it in a letter that may or may not be mailed.

Discussing Your Feelings About The Past

When you are ready, share your feelings about the past with the person you have chosen. Doing so will help you resolve any guilt and shame you may feel about it. You will achieve a sense of completion that will help you get on with your life. When you share your past, you will most often find that your listener has also felt those feelings and has had similar experiences as well. Most of us think our experiences and feelings are unique to us. Sharing them with another and attending a support group will enable you to see that what you've felt and experienced is typical of adult children.

Madeline: When I was little, I used to think that I was the only one whose father got drunk and abused her. I used to think I was the only one who cried at night. When I grew up, I thought I was the only one whose husband didn't talk to her, who hit her. Going to meetings has let me see how common what's happened to me is, and that my feelings — all the anger I feel — are shared by most of the women there, by millions of women. Somehow, I feel better for knowing that.

When And If To Share Feelings

Identifying your feelings and knowing how to express them does not obligate you to do so. Since you don't have to take action, there is no risk in learning how to do so. You have nothing to be afraid of.

Before you express your feelings, you need to use dual perspective and ask yourself how you would respond if you were on the receiving end of those feelings. Consider the possible consequences of expressing your feelings and ask yourself if you would be willing to live with those consequences.

For example, sharing intimate details of your past may overwhelm someone on a first date and cause him or her to back off. Your boss may not appreciate your reactions to his management style and may penalize you. Your mother may be devastated by your angry letter and refuse to see you. Consider the ninth step of AA, which encourages you to make amends, except when to do so would harm yourself or others. Having the skills to identify and express your feelings gives you choices. How, when, and in what way you exercise those choices leaves you in control of your life.

3

Active Listening

My 11th grader, Jack, came home dragging his feet. "That damn teacher," he grumbled.

"You sound upset," I said.

"Well I am," he replied. "I got a 'D' on my first English exam."

Now normally, I would have reassured Jack ("I'm sure you can do better than that!"). Or I'd have denied that any problem existed at all ("When I was your age, I once got a 'D' on the first exam, and I ended up with an 'A'!"). But I had just learned active listening, and all I said was, "You seem worried." Boy, that *really* opened him up!

"Yeah, I *am*, Mom," he confided. "I'm worried I might flunk the class, worried I might not get into a good college . . . worried I might disappoint you." We talked for an hour. I didn't judge him. I didn't advise him. I just used active listening. I learned so much about him. I felt closer to him than I have in years.

— *Sandra*

Active listening is a remarkable skill for letting others know you are paying attention, for encouraging them to open up, for understanding others. Many psychologists consider it the most valuable skill you can learn for relating well, the "missing link" in most people's ability to communicate. Yet for all its acclaim, active listening is practically unknown. Simply stated, *active listening is putting into words your understanding of what the other person has said*. The following five-step formula will show you exactly how to use this most valuable skill:

1. Pay careful attention to the other person, listening for messages that seem emotionally charged or important. ("You told me you'd be here at 3:00 and here it is, 4:30!")

2. Ask yourself, "What is this person feeling?" or "What is this person saying?" Which question you ask will depend on whether the emotions behind the words or the words themselves seem the most important.

3. Briefly share with the other person your answer to one of the questions in Step 2. ("You sound angry.") Don't add judgments or criticism. ("You *shouldn't* be angry.") Your goal in active listening is simply to let the other person know you have heard the message. Be careful not to tell others how they feel; simply tell them what it seems like to you.

4. The other person will probably both tell you that you are right and expand on the subject. ("Yes I am. I just sat there doing nothing while I waited.") If you are wrong, the other person will most likely correct you. ("No, I'm not angry. I spent the time while I waited working on projects that needed attention anyhow.")

5. Especially if your original active listening proved inaccurate, you may want to try again, active listening to the response you got in Step 4. ("So my being late wasn't a great inconvenience for you.") Or you may want to go back to Step 1 and wait for another opportunity.

Here are some more examples of how this skill works:

Irv: I'm sorry we went to visit my mom.
Margaret: [Active listening.] You seem angry.
Irv: I am. The way she tried to force me to eat more food, the way she asked me if I've "finally" found a job I can hold . . .
Margaret: [Active listening.] You think she treats you like a child.
Irv: Right. I'm 35, for goodness sake!

Mona: I've been on hold for 15 minutes.
Jane: [Active listening.] You must feel pretty frustrated.
Mona: Yeah, I feel like they don't really care how long they keep me waiting.

Active Listening With Children

Active listening is especially valuable when you talk with children. While judging and criticizing them will shut down the lines of communication, active listening opens them up. Most of the time, when you use this skill with children, you will want to focus on their feelings, as in the following examples:

Child: Bobbie lied to me.
Parent: [Active listening.] Sounds like you're mad at Bobbie.
Child: Yeah, she said she'd give me her ring, and she didn't.
Parent: [Active listening.] She went back on her word.
Child: Right, and now I'm not gonna be her friend!

Child: I wish I was never born.
Parent: [Active listening.] You're pretty upset.
Child: Yeah, Sally invited everyone to her birthday party except me.

Child: I got on base twice in the ball game today.
Parent: [Active listening.] You must be really excited.
Child: Yup, and what's more, the second time I got a run in!

Child: I don't feel like eating tonight.
Parent: [Active listening.] You sound unhappy.
Child: Yeah, I don't have any friends at school.
Parent: [Active listening.] You must feel lonely during recess and at lunch.
Child: And after school. Today I invited Ozzie to come over here — and he said no.

Parent: [Active listening.] You're disappointed.
Child: Yeah, and I feel like I'm *never* gonna have any friends.
Parent: [Active listening.] Like you'll be alone forever.
Child: Right.

Active Listening Helps You Understand Others

Active listening can help you be certain you have accurately received messages. Since you are not a mind reader, you can never be certain of the thoughts and feelings of others. You depend on signals — the words others say and how they say them — to tell you what they are thinking and how they are feeling. Frequently these signals are ambiguous; the same signal may have many possible meanings. Active listening can be invaluable in situations like these in helping you avoid misunderstandings and arriving at the truth. When you put into words your understanding of what others say, they will be able either to affirm that you are correct or to set you straight. For example:

Brad: Don't go to your 12-Step meeting tonight.
Cynthia: [Active listening.] You don't like me working on my program.
Brad: It's not that. It's just that I feel lonely and I'd like you to be with me tonight.

Randy: Do we have to invite the Gallagers over so soon?
Sharon: [Active listening.] You don't like them.
Randy: I *do* like them, but I've got too much work to do this week.

Peggy: I've decided to quit my job.
Barbara: [Active listening.] You don't like being a typist.
Peggy: You got it. I don't know if I can do better, but I know I can't do worse.

Active Listening Helps Keep Your Conversations Going

Adult children frequently complain that they have difficulty keeping their conversations going. They say that awkward silence always seems to be just around the corner. Your using active listening, like your asking open questions and talking about yourself, will help. Active listening promotes a warm, supportive climate that encourages others to feel comfortable, open up, and speak freely.

Not only will active listening help others talk more, it will help you as well. If you have difficulty thinking of things to say, you are probably trying to talk both to the other person and to yourself at the same time. This self-talk, most of which consists of worrying about what to say next and "catastrophizing" about all the "terrible" things that might go wrong, distracts your attention and makes it nearly impossible for you to follow the train of the conversation. Active listening requires so much attention that you will tend to ignore your self-talk in favor of getting deeply involved in the conversation. With your mind clear of distractions, thoughts and ideas will come more easily. And after you've given your listeners a good hearing, chances are they'll be even more eager to hear what you have to say too!

Typical Problems With Active Listening

Not Identifying Feelings

If you have difficulty identifying what your conversational partner is feeling, use dual perspective by picturing yourself in her situation and asking yourself, "How would I be feeling?" If that doesn't work, picture a time when you had a similar type of experience and recall how you felt. Suppose, for example, that a friend is describing how nervous she felt testifying in court. If you have testified in court, recall how you felt. If you haven't, think about how you felt giving a speech in public, talking to your boss, starting a conversation with an attractive member of the opposite sex. Evoking similar images may well help you get in touch with similar emotions.

Focusing Only On Content

Many adult children do a great job reflecting the content of messages but ignore the feelings behind them. The problem with this is that emotions are frequently the most important part of the message. "I told my husband how much I'd enjoyed my job," a student once said, "but what I wanted him to get was how shattering it was to lose it." Especially when strong feelings are involved, most people will feel you have missed the point if you ignore the emotions they feel.

Using the information and exercises in Chapter 2, as you get better at identifying and expressing emotions, you will find it easier to use active listening to reflect other people's feelings.

Some adult children ignore or downplay the negative emotions others express, figuring they'll go away.

Child: I was mad when you didn't show up for my game.
Parent: You were a little upset.

Exactly the opposite is true. Acknowledging the feelings of others has a cathartic effect on them, while ignoring their feelings tends to intensify them.

Repeating Messages

Beginners to active listening often merely repeat or reword the things they hear. For example:

Denise: I'm upset.
Sandy: You're upset.
Denise: I wish my mother would let me live my own life.
Sandy: You want her to leave you alone.
Denise: I wish she'd understand that I'm grown up now.
Sandy: You'd like her to know that you're grown up.

Simple repeating the responses of others usually only annoys them. Real active listening requires that you add your own thoughts as to what others feel and mean.

Offering Criticism Or Advice

Active listening consists of simply mirroring back to others what their messages mean to you. This is no simple task in our Western culture. We are strongly conditioned when we see or hear *anything* to judge it: good or bad;

A, B, C, D or F; healthy or unhealthy; fashionable or unfashionable; 1 to 10; expensive or cheap; thumbs up or down. Similarly, we are conditioned, when we hear problems, to offer "solutions." Often, however, people who tell you their problems don't want your judgment, don't want your advice. All they want is simply to be heard. As Dr. Bernie Siegel writes of his son in his book, *Love, Medicine & Miracles:* "Recently, as a teenager, when he came home with problems, his father had solutions like love, accept, forgive, but he said, 'I don't need answers. I need someone to listen.' When we play the role of a saint with one-word answers, we don't help people. We help when we listen and share our pain."

Active Listening To Body Language

Body language is even more open to misinterpretation than spoken language. The same nonverbal sign (such as a smile, a frown, or crossed legs) may signify a variety of emotions. We all draw conclusions based upon these signs, and our conclusions are frequently wrong. For this reason, it is often wise to check out our conclusions, using the following three-step formula:

1. State what you saw and heard that leads you to your conclusion.

2. State your conclusion. Be sure to do this in a *tentative* manner, making it clear that the other person will be the final judge.

3. Ask if your conclusion is what was intended.

For example:

"When I suggested just now that we buy that 'Incredible Self-Confidence' video, you said, 'Fine,' but you frowned. I think you don't want me to buy it. Am I right?"

"When I asked if I might house-sit while you're gone, you said, 'We'll see' and changed the subject. I think you'd rather not have me house-sit. Am I right?"

"You keep looking at your watch as we're talking and I think you'd like me to go now. Am I right?"

If you have not yet come to a conclusion, simply state what you saw and heard and ask the other person for an explanation. For example:

"You crossed your arms and changed the subject when I suggested we drop by to have me meet your parents. Is something the matter?"

"The smile left your face when you looked at the check. What's up?"

"When I asked you how your ACoA meeting went, you turned red. I'm curious to know why."

4

Asking For What You Want

I sometimes think I've wasted most of my life waiting and hoping. When I was growing up, I always hoped some teacher would notice how troubled I was and would somehow help me and my family. That never happened. When I was looking for a job, I hoped friends would see my problem and help me. They gave me sympathy, but no help. When I was married, I always figured my husband would somehow know when I needed a hug or a shoulder to cry on. And it didn't work. It was all such a waste, all that waiting and hoping. Now I'm older and I know better. Now, when I want something, *I ask*.

— *Mollie*

Passively pretending everything is okay while hoping others will give you what you want hardly ever works. People can't read your mind and so they've no way of knowing what it is you want — or that you want anything.

Hinting is only somewhat more likely to get you any help. When you hint that you'd like some help by saying that your car is acting up or that you're feeling down, other people are unlikely to get the hint. If by chance they do, they're still not likely to think that the problem is of much importance to you. Aggressively demanding that others give you what you want does get your point across. But it causes others to resist giving you what you want, or to give it only grudgingly and on a short-term basis. When you look at all the options, it becomes obvious that *the best way to get what you want is to assertively ask for it.*

Figuring Out What You Want

Before you can ask for what you want, you have to know what you want. Sometimes this will be obvious, while at other times you may want to go through the following steps:

Ask yourself, *"What am I saying to myself?"* and write down the answer. Your thoughts, which can be called your self-talk, will often tell you exactly what you want and don't want. Sonya, for example, had been living with an acquaintance who wanted her to sign a full year's lease. She had put off signing, but she wasn't really in touch with why. It was only when she wrote down her self-talk during the day, silent inner messages like, "I hate her music" and "I wish her friends wouldn't hang around," that she fully understood that she wanted to find another place to live.

If you find it difficult to get in touch with your self-talk, quiet down and ask yourself, "What am I feeling?" and write down the answer. Most of the time, the feelings you write down will give you important clues to what you want. If you're feeling angry, for example, you may well want to ask someone to do or to stop doing something. If you're feeling lonely, you probably want to invite someone to join you in some activity. Be concrete about what you want. What will it look like? What exactly will happen?

When? Be aware, as you decide what you want, that you will most likely feel at least a little ambivalent about every choice. For example, deciding to see a movie with one person means spending time and perhaps money, and means passing up other people and activities that might turn out to be more enjoyable.

> *Alan:* This was one of the most important insights of my life. When I graduated from college, I looked around for a career, but every one I looked into had drawbacks. I wanted a girl-friend, but no one was in every way exactly what I wanted. I looked around for an apartment of my own, but none was perfect. As a result, I went many years with no job or with menial jobs, with no woman, living with parents I couldn't relate to. It was only when I realized that nobody and nothing would ever be perfect and that I'd always be a little ambivalent about everything, that I started making progress in my life.

The following additional exercises may also help you get in touch with what you want.

EXERCISE: Pretend that a friend is in your shoes. Ask yourself what this friend, looking at your life, would want from others. Then decide to be a friend to yourself and ask for those things.

> *Lori:* A friend looking at me a month ago would say, "Ask your kids to get themselves ready in the morning. Ask your husband to go out on the town with you more." I did that, and my children have been surprisingly good, for the most part, about helping. And my husband . . . our Friday night dates have become the highlight of my week.

EXERCISE: As you go through the day, write down the situations in which you feel the most hurried, the most stressed. At the end of the day, think about those times and write out how others might help make them easier. Then ask for their help.

Alicia: I found myself most stressed in the morning, when I'd be running like mad to get myself and the children washed and dressed and fed and ready for the day. I decided the only way to unstress the situation was to get up and get started half an hour earlier and get to bed half an hour earlier. At first I resented this because it meant missing Johnny Carson's monologue, but I solved that problem by taping him. With a little effort and a little rearranging, instead of being the worst time of my day, now my mornings are often the best.

EXERCISE: Write out a list of things you enjoy doing with others. If you can't think of several, add to your list activities you have enjoyed doing with others in times past. Chances are you'd still enjoy doing them today. Then, every few days, ask someone to do one of those things with you.

Linda: Going over my list, I realized how long it had been since our family had gone on a trip together, played cards together, had a picnic together, even eaten dinner with everyone there. I'd been telling myself that's just how teenagers are, but now I've invited them to an old-fashioned picnic — and they're all excited!

Making Requests

Once you know what you want, the next step is to ask for it. You may want to write out your requests beforehand, so you'll be sure you've phrased them in the most effective way possible. And you may find it helpful to roleplay, making your requests first to a friend, or to tape them and listen to how you sound. Whether you practice beforehand or not, consider the following in making your requests:

Use dual perspective. Think not just in terms of what you want, but also in terms of those you ask. Do they appear to have time to listen to your requests? If you're not sure, ask: "Have you got a minute free?" Do they appear to have the ability to help you? Once again, if you're not sure, ask: "Do you know anything about fixing cars?" "Do you know how to use a computer?" Are they likely to be interested or at least willing to grant your request? Some friends, for example, enjoy driving and may think nothing of taking you to the airport; for others driving that far would be an unpleasant chore.

Be direct. Let others know exactly what you want of them and when you want it: "Will you look over my report today and correct my spelling?"

Give your reasons. Telling others *why* you are making the request will increase your chances of getting help: "Please help me fold these clothes. I've got an Al-Anon meeting to go to at seven." "I could sure use your help with this math problem. It'll be on tomorrow's exam." "Will you give me a ride to General Electric? I've got a job interview and my car's on the blink." When you tell someone why you are making the request, you may get an added bonus. They may be able to suggest a better solution or help you in unexpected ways: "My uncle works at GE. Maybe he can help you land that job."

> *Bonnie:* One night I said to my boys, "I'm really tired and I need some help. So what about the dishes?"
>
> To my surprise, Tyler spoke right up to Robert, "I'll take Tuesday and Thursday; you have Monday and Wednesday."
>
> Robert said, "Monday is fine, but I have practice Wednesday. Could I have Monday and Tuesday?"
>
> Tyler said, "That's fine. Do you want to feed the dog the same night or different?" I couldn't believe what I was hearing!

Appeal to others' self-interest. If you can, show those you ask how they would benefit by helping you. People are more likely to do something if it's clear that they would profit as well. "If you'll drop off this package, you'll get to meet Becky." "If you'll drive me to the gym, I'll get you a guest pass to come in and work out." The benefit you mention does not have to follow directly from the favor; you can propose a trade-off: "If you'll help me paint my nails, I'll help you study for your exam." "If you'll drive me to the airport, I'll owe you a big favor any time you ask." Use dual perspective in this; the benefit you offer must be important to the other person. A guest pass to a gym may mean nothing to someone who doesn't value exercise.

Issuing Invitations

The most common requests you make will probably be invitations. Regularly issuing invitations will enable you to counter directly the sad tendency of many adult children to isolate themselves. The general strategies we've outlined for making requests all apply to issuing invitations. With people you don't know well, here are two additional strategies that will help make it more likely that you'll get a yes.

Start small. When you issue an invitation, especially for the first time, start small. You'd be more likely to give someone ten minutes of your time than a full evening, wouldn't you? Well, the same is true of other people. The less time and expense and effort you ask for, the more likely they are to say yes. So when you issue your invitations, *start small*, and you'll probably succeed.

> *Barbara:* When I'd meet someone at Step study, I used to invite them to my house for dinner, but only about half would accept. Now I just suggest getting a cup of coffee afterward — and they almost always say yes.

Starting small is an especially good strategy if you are a woman who feels uncomfortable about issuing invitations. When you invite someone to go for a walk or to have tea with you, it's almost as though you haven't issued an invitation at all. And if you get turned down, neither of you will think it's any big deal.

Sound casual. How you issue your invitations shapes the responses you get more than you might think. Make them sound like your life is on the line and you're likely to scare others away. Sound casual and present your invitations simply as opportunities to have a good time and they'll have a far greater chance of being accepted.

INSTEAD OF SAYING . . .	SAY . . .
You're probably busy, but . . . I've enjoyed meeting you and I thought that maybe — if you don't mind — we could spend Saturday together.	I'm enjoying our chat. Let's continue over a cup of coffee.

Andrew: I got to know the woman who is now my wife by starting small and sounding casual, just like you said. We met at a business meeting, and a few days later I phoned and ever so casually announced that I was in the area and would like to drop off some papers. She agreed. When I came by, we talked about the papers — and about lots more besides. We found we had plenty in common, and we found we enjoyed each other's company.

If You Get A "No"

When you ask for what you want, most of the time you will get a "Yes." When you are turned down, propose an alternative, taking into account any objections the other person may have raised.

Cynthia: Would you drive me to the airport at 12:30 tomorrow afternoon? I'll buy you lunch on the way.
Ann: Gosh, I'd like to, but I'll be busy all afternoon.
Cynthia: How about late morning then?

Should you once again be turned down, you may choose to conclude that the other person isn't interested. If so, tell them, "Sorry you can't make it" or "Well, I've enjoyed meeting you." On the other hand you may decide to persist.

> *Diane:* We met a couple on a cruise, and every few months, when we were in the D.C. area, we'd call to see if they were free. The first four or five times, they weren't, though they encouraged us to try again. I wasn't sure if they were putting us on, but I figured, "What do I have to lose?" Finally, one time they were free, we did get together, and it was great. I'm glad I didn't listen to that little voice saying, "They don't really like you. They were just being nice to you on the cruise."

If you don't get what you want, congratulate yourself for speaking up and making the effort. Tell yourself that, just as you have the right to ask, others have the right to decline. Don't take turndowns personally. There are 31 flavors of ice cream in the store precisely because people have different tastes. The fact that they don't have the time or that you don't match their taste says something about them but absolutely nothing about you. Let a few people get to know you and chances are good that you'll find some who like you just fine.

If You Get A "Yes"

When your requests or invitations are accepted, resist the temptation to ask others if they *really* want to do you the favor or join you in the activity. That may lead them to reconsider and may snatch defeat out of the jaws of victory. Instead, silently congratulate yourself for being assertive, smile, and *enjoy*.

5

Giving Others What They Want

Golden Rule variation: Do unto others as *they* would
have you do unto them. Rationale: Very often others
don't want what you want.

— *Richard C. Huseman, Ph.D.*

As an adult child, you most likely have difficulty giving
to others what they want. This chapter will provide you
with guidelines you can use.

Use dual perspective: Tailor what you offer others to their
needs and wants. Put yourself in their shoes and ask:
"Based on what I know about them, what would they
respond to?" "What might they enjoy having?" "What
would be a help to them?"

Observe and listen: The best way to get dual perspective
and offer that which will be appreciated is sometimes to
observe and listen to others.

Beth: The first day of our vacation, I noticed that Harry
was hopping in pain as he walked from his car to the sand

— the asphalt was *that hot!* I sneaked away later and bought him thongs. They only cost $5, but he was so grateful. I think it was more that I noticed his problem and cared enough to help.

Marlene: My mother often complained she couldn't find a potato peeler that worked. Just couldn't find one. So on my last trip to Europe, I bought her one or two peelers in every country I visited. She roared when I presented them to her! Said it was the best present she's received in years!

Observing and listening to others works, even when they know what you are doing:

Peter: Rather than give Anne money to buy an engagement ring (which would tell her I don't much care), or springing one on her (and risk getting one she didn't like), I invited her to go looking at rings with me. I observed what she liked and what she *really* liked, and bought her one of those. She was pleased with my choice, but she told me what made the gift truly wonderful was my taking the time and effort to learn her taste.

Ask: Perhaps the best way to take the guesswork out of giving is simply to ask the other person what he wants: "Your birthday is next week and I want to get you something. Do you have an idea what you would like?" Or, ask the other person if he wants to be surprised or would rather be sure that the present you're considering would be welcome. If he says he doesn't care about being surprised, then say, "I'm thinking about getting you _____. Would you like that?" True, the element of surprise is gone, but that may be important to you and not him.

Give yourself: The greatest gifts you can give won't cost you anything and can't be put in a box. They are your expressions of love and appreciation, your encouragement, and your assistance. Here too, use dual perspective in deciding what to say and do.

Henry: My niece wrote down my birthday in her datebook, and every May 8, she sends me a handmade card wishing me a Happy Birthday and saying she loves me. Most times it's the only card I get.

Louise: A friend from Al-Anon told the group that she had been fired that day from her job. I asked myself, what would I want to hear if I were she, and I told her — and I really meant it — that I believed in her and that anyone who would fire her was a fool. Months later, she told me she had thought about what I had said many times, and it had really helped her bounce back.

Georgia: One summer, my father saw that I didn't have anything to do. He asked me if it was okay with me if he helped me out, and when I said I was desperate and could use all the help I could get, he called up a friend of his and got me a job. I've always loved him for that.

Giving to manipulate: Adult children often give for highly manipulative reasons. They will give in order to keep others around. They are, in effect, trying to buy friendship. They devote so much time and energy and money to that goal that they end up resenting others because they can never pay back enough. Also, they resent others for "making" them give, for "victimizing" them (when in reality they were volunteers, not victims). For this reason, Rick Potter, the Director of Safe Harbor at Costa Mesa, California, says the ACoA dance goes:

> *Give, give, give, resent.*
> *Give, give, give, resent.*

The problem with this strategy (aside from the fact that it leaves you resentful, impoverished, and exhausted) is that it doesn't work. When you give others so much more than they give you, they will typically feel guilty. When you give it with so many strings attached, they will typically feel resentful. As they get weaker and weaker from doing nothing while you do everything, far from being eternally grateful, they will often respond by making your life miserable. And if they have enough internal strength left, they may well leave you.

One thing they are highly unlikely to do is love you. W. W. Broadbent, M.D., notes that in researching his book, *How To Be Loved,* he searched for that extra something those who were loved had or did. He found none.

What he did find was one thing those who were loved seldom did: They seldom tried to manipulate others in order to be accepted. Those who were unloved, however, were endlessly trying to manipulate others to approve of them, accept them and love them.

There is no easy answer to controlling manipulative behavior. The first step is to realize that the rewards of giving it up are far greater than the rewards of continuing it. The idea is to give without having strings attached. Give because it gives you pleasure to do so without expectation. By the same token, you can receive a gesture of thoughtfulness and just enjoy it without any obligation on your part. The second step is to recognize when you are being manipulative. And the third step is to cut down the frequency of those times. These steps are best undertaken in therapy and in conjunction with participation in support groups.

6

Solving Problems

Sally felt trapped. She had spent the last eight years typing classified ads into a computer for a major newspaper. "Hour after hour, day after day, I type in fascinating copy like, 'Echo Par Fem. sks same for nu 1 br apt. $325.' Sometimes I fantasize I'm lounging on the beach in Florida or Hawaii, the sun warming me, gentle breezes massaging me — and then I come back to reality and find I'm typing, '1976 Colt, 4 dr. New clutch. Orig. ownr.' Other times, I dream I'm working with children. I *love* to play with children. I suppose I could do it for real, become a pre-school teacher or a playground leader. But the darn money at the paper, it's just *so* good." Lately Sally has been feeling more hopeless and depressed. "They try to make it seem like we're a team, like putting out this paper is a real cause. But it's been getting harder and harder. Eight hours of this seems more like a year."

Marsha felt miserable about living with her mother. "I'm 34, too old to have to put up with her criticizing my friends, listening in on my calls, and opening my mail. The other night I was out on the town, and when I came home, my mother was sitting in the kitchen waiting up for me! I couldn't believe it! I just started yelling at her that I want her to let me live my own life! I'd move out, but I can't afford it. Besides, what if she needed help in the middle of the night . . . ? I've heard of women passing their whole lives with their mothers. I don't want to be one of them, but I see that's what's happening."

Lauren liked the *idea* of marrying the president of a company. It was the *reality* that she couldn't stand. "Now I know why wealthy men are wealthy," she said. "They work *all* the time. He leaves home by eight, just as I'm waking up. He's gone till six, seven, eight, sometimes later. I have a nice home, pretty clothes and enough money, but I feel like a widow. I feel . . . empty."

Like Sally, Marsha and Lauren, you often feel locked into situations. You cling tenaciously to unhealthy relationships, living situations and jobs. If you grew up in a dysfunctional family, you had no model for solving problems. Problems got compounded but never resolved. They would get ignored but would come up time and time again. You became expert at handling crisis situations, but you never saw how a problem could be dealt with so that it didn't reach crisis proportions. The systematic solution to a problem that is described here is not a part of your experience. Chances are that as a result of your history, you are using one or more of the following dysfunctional ways of handling your problems.

Upholding the status quo: Although you don't like the way things are, you see no possibility for change and so carry on as always. Even if you do see possibilities for change, you do nothing because you fear losing what control you have. Besides, the status quo does have *some* rewards, and you don't want to risk losing those — unsatisfying though they are.

Denial: You still observe the "no talk" rule of your childhood and pretend everything is all right. If others ask you worried questions, you pretend you are happy and deny your problems exist. You may even be denying your problems to yourself.

Waiting for a miracle: You may be telling yourself that your problems will magically disappear — when you meet Mr. or Ms. Right, when you win the lottery, when you leave home, when you get a raise. If any of these hoped-for events do take place, you are disappointed that your problems don't all disappear. And you wait expectantly for the next miracle.

Waiting for others: You may be hoping that others will notice your plight and help you without being asked. But others are not telepathic. They can't read your mind. Since you don't tell them your problems, they have no way of knowing what you want or even that you want anything.

Blaming/complaining: You may be spending time assigning blame to others for your problems and ignoring any responsibility on your part. Or, you may be laying the blame at your own doorstep, even when you had little to do with the situation. When you spend time complaining, you feel better temporarily, but your griping ultimately lowers your self-esteem, costs you friends — and doesn't change anything.

Creating a crisis: You either behave impulsively or aggravate the situation to crisis proportions in order to make the situation familiar and reduce your anxiety.

Chances are that many of the ways you handle problems today are the same ways you handled them in your childhood. When you were growing up, you were helpless to solve your family's problems. But today you have a vast array of options — if you will only recognize and pursue them. You may think that you are stuck, but change is always possible.

The Reverend Robert Schuller exemplifies the kind of attitude that, if practiced one day at a time, can help you get unstuck:

> When faced with a mountain,
> *I will not quit!* I will keep
> on striving until I climb

over, find a pass through,
tunnel underneath — or
simply stay and turn the
mountain into a gold mine,
with God's help.

A Formula For Solving Problems

Problem-solving is a process. It involves a number of steps. Although some problems may appear to solve themselves, and some problems, when put into perspective, may be easily resolved, there is still a process that goes on. A conscious awareness of the process and an active involvement in it will help you feel more in charge of your life. The steps are:

1. Identify the problem.
2. Decide to solve the problem.
3. Brainstorm possible solutions.
4. Decide on the best alternative.
5. Decide how to implement the plan.
6. Carry out the plan.
7. Hold a follow-up meeting.

Identify The Problem

Sometimes you may be only generally aware that things aren't right but unsure of what the problem is. At these times focus more attention on the situation, and the problem will often become evident: "Brad came home an hour late and didn't phone." "Eric didn't clean up his toys." "Sylvie called at seven this morning and woke me up."

If your problem is harder to identify, look for any evidence your body may provide. When you feel anxious, depressed, or lethargic, ask yourself what you were doing before, during, or after experiencing those feelings. If need be, record your feelings and the situations that surround them for a number of days to clarify the situation.

Lauren, for example, first became aware of how unhappy she was with her life when she began keeping a journal. She noted that she felt headachy and on the verge of sleep several times a day. She noted that most of her shopping was done merely to fill up time, to fill up the emptiness inside her. "Before," she observed, "I had told myself I 'should' be happy to be married to such a successful man. But now I realize I'm really not happy at all."

Next, *decide if the problem is yours.* Adult children often confuse other people's problems with their own. As a result, they waste time, effort and money in impossible efforts to solve other people's problems. A problem is yours when *you* are the person whose needs and desires are not being met. When a friend switches your TV show, when a roommate fails to keep a promise to help you, when neighbors disturb you with loud noise, the problem is yours. Why? Because the friend, roommate, and neighbors are getting their needs satisfied, but you aren't.

In the following situations, the problem is *not* yours:

- A friend is overworked and underpaid.
- An uncle has lost his job.
- A nephew has to cancel a vacation because he doesn't have enough money.
- An aunt is getting a divorce.
- A friend is having difficulty collecting a loan.
- Your neighbors are having marital difficulties.
- A relative wants a ride to the airport.
- A friend is upset because you haven't called lately.
- A friend feels lonely.
- A co-worker got his car back from the garage — and it still doesn't work.

You may wish these people well in resolving their problems, but it is important to recognize that the problems are *theirs* and *not yours.*

Once you are aware that solving a given problem is *not* your responsibility, you have choices:

1. You can walk away from it.
2. You can offer to be a good listener.

3. You can offer to share a similar experience in your own life and tell how you resolved it for yourself.
4. You can make a greater effort to reach out during what you know is a difficult time.
5. You can participate in the solution, e.g., offer to drive your relative to the airport even though you know it is not your obligation to do so.

To sum up, if it is not your problem, tell yourself that you don't have to lend support to everyone with a problem and that, even if you choose to help, in most cases people are able and prefer to solve their own problems.

If the problem *is* yours, *define it in writing*. Work on your definition until you get it right. Be sure to include the role that *you* play in the problem. Finding out how you are part of the problem will help you in the following steps to see how you can be part of the solution. For example, people whose social lives are dull or nonexistent often neglect to consider the role they play in this state of affairs. Most typically, they will not even show up at events that give them the opportunity to meet people. When they do show up, they normally wear a blank face. They stand around waiting for others to introduce themselves. Anyone who sees them, of course, will assume they aren't interested and will spend their time with people who appear more welcoming.

Define your problem in terms of *needs*, not solutions. When Sally, for example, defined her problem in terms of solutions, she said, "I want to get away from the newspaper." But when she defined her problem in terms of needs, she realized, "I need a job doing work I consider meaningful, a job in some way involving children." Defining her problem in terms of needs led her to seek out a part-time job as a pre-school teacher after work and, eventually, to open up her own day-care service out of her home. "I currently have five little ones," she said. "I make a little less money, but I'm a million times happier."

When another person is involved, defining your problem in terms of needs is more likely to result in solutions that satisfy both of you. For example: Sandy wanted to spend her week's vacation exploring Vermont and New Hampshire by car. Her companion, Richard, wanted to sunbathe on St. John in the Virgin Islands. When they held fast to their positions and argued back and forth about which was better, they felt frustrated and angry at each other, and got nowhere. They did considerably better when they dropped their positions and instead asked themselves, "What do I want from a vacation?" They both found that what they wanted was to get away from city traffic, from clocks, from office responsibilities. They both wanted to relax and see a few sights. By getting off their positions and viewing their problem this way, they discovered dozens of acceptable options, and it was far easier for them to arrive at a mutually satisfying solution.

Here's another example: A week before Julie and Hans were scheduled to move 65 miles away, Julie decided to buy a computer table at a garage sale. Hans argued against it, not wanting to have one more thing to pay the movers for. Julie argued that she didn't want them to go on using the shaky old table they presently used, and she was afraid they would if they didn't get a new one right away when they moved in. Their fighting carried on for several days — until they finally decided to get off their positions and consider their wants and needs. Both agreed they wanted a new table when they moved to their new house, and neither wanted to pay more money to the movers. So they agreed that the day after they moved to their new home, they would take steps to find and buy a new table. Julie was happy — she was getting her new table. And Hans was happy — he was avoiding extra moving expenses.

Decide To Solve The Problem

A key question to ask yourself before you go on to the next step is: Is the energy involved in solving the problem worth the effort? Suppose, for example, that Susan's housekeeper does not follow her instructions. Is it worth Susan's time and energy to train her, or should she let her go? An excellent way to decide is to list the pros and cons.

PROS	CONS
1. She knows the house.	1. The house isn't clean.
2. She is honest.	2. I am upset by her work.
3. She is reasonable.	3. I end up doing most of the work myself.

Looking over and weighing the pros and cons, you will often find that the right decision becomes apparent. If Susan decides that, no, it is not worth the effort to train the housekeeper, she would, at this point, stop and fire her. If she decides that, yes, it is worth the effort, she would then continue with the process outlined here.

If you are ambivalent and cannot make a decision, go through the rest of this process as an exercise. Then see if making a decision to go forward becomes easier. One last point: Beware of making decisions based on momentary feelings (e.g., how tired you feel right now). Instead, decide on the basis of what makes the most sense in the long run. Most decisions are judgment calls. You can never know with 100 percent certainty that you have made the right decision until after the decision is made. However, making a decision, right or wrong, is preferable to being passive and letting life happen to you. There are some who argue that making no decision is, in itself, a decision. It is. It is a decision to give up charge of your life.

Brainstorm Possible Solutions

Once you have defined your problem, it's time to brainstorm possible solutions. Brainstorming is coming up with as many solutions as you possibly can without pausing to evaluate them. Look at the problem upside down, sideways, and backwards. Think of practical and routine ways to solve your problem — and ridiculous, wild, crazy ways to solve your problem. Pretend a friend has asked you for help with this problem. What would you recommend? Imagine yourself with $1,000,000 in the bank. How would you solve it then? If you had only one year to live, what would you do about this problem then?

Possible solutions can often be broken down into changes in *behavior* (Marsha could learn to be assertive in asking her mother not to open her mail), *situation* (she could move out), or *attitude* (even if Marsha couldn't change her behavior or her mother's, even if she couldn't change the situation, she could still change her attitude toward the situation. For example, she could start seeing her mother less as a tormentor and more as an eccentric, lonely old woman who loves her dearly).

As you come up with possible solutions, pause just long enough to write them down. When critical thoughts come to mind — reasons why particular solutions won't work — pay those thoughts no attention. Instead, simply go back to thinking up new ideas. If you do a good job, most of your ideas will be silly or impractical, but using this method will often enable you to come up with unique and creative ideas. Be certain that among the options you come up with is the option to do nothing and to simply keep doing what you are doing. That is a very real possibility — and occasionally the best one.

Beware of telling yourself early on that you've thought of everything possible, when you've only thought of a few obvious options. Adult children often do that, and that's one reason they often see themselves as trapped. Stick with it, perhaps over several days, and you will almost always discover you have lots of options.

———————————————■———————————————

EXERCISE: Pick a problem of yours and decide what you could do to make it even worse. For example, if your problem is that you have no close friends and feel lonely, ask yourself, "What could I do to be *totally* alone?" or "What can I do to keep people even *more* distant?" Some answers might be, "Never go out to places where there is a risk of meeting someone," "Never smile at anyone," or "Never talk about myself or express interest in others." This will give you some clues as to what you are presently doing wrong and what you might do to solve the problem.

You may find it helpful to find one or more people to brainstorm with. If these people are genuinely interested in working with you on a solution, brainstorming with them may help you arrive at solutions even better than those you would find on your own. They may build on each other's ideas, either by improving on one or by combining two. As Napoleon Hill wrote in his famed book, *Think and Grow Rich*, "A group of brains coordinated (or connected) in a spirit of harmony will provide more thought-energy than a single brain, just as a group of electric batteries will provide more energy than a single battery."

In your brainstorming session, as people come up with new ideas, write them down, but don't write down who suggested them. The goal of brainstorming is not to have *your* idea adopted but to have the *best* idea adopted. Everyone can take credit for a job well done.

Before Marsha began brainstorming, she was certain she had no alternative but to endure living with her mother. A friend she invited to brainstorm with her challenged the two of them to find no less than ten alternatives. This is what their brainstorming list looked like:

- Move in with a friend and share rent.
- Find a roommate who lives near your mother.
- Sleep on a friend's couch.
- Draw boundaries with your mother.
- Continue living with mother.
- Get a higher paying job.
- Get a second job.
- Become a live-in maid for somebody.

- Arrange for mother to have another woman move in, so she won't be alone.
- Arrange for mother to have a safety alarm to alert an ambulance in case of emergency. Then move to Africa.
- Move to Atlanta.
- Move to Germany.
- Join the Army.
- Become a house-sitter.
- Get married.
- Join the Peace Corps.
- Buy a camper and live in it.
- Move to Spain and teach English.

Once Marsha and her friend got started brainstorming, she discovered she had *hundreds* of options, almost every one of which was preferable to her present situation.

Decide On The Best Alternative

Look at your brainstorming list, giving due consideration to ideas that are creative or unusual. Select the alternative that seems to do the best job of solving the problem while offering the fewest drawbacks. If you are brainstorming with others, ask each person to select the alternative they believe best solves the problem. Look first at any options that more than one person has selected, as those will frequently be the best ones. Discuss their relative merits and shortcomings, looking for long-term rewards and not just short-term gratification. Others may have their say, but if you own the problem, you have the final say. If the group owns the problem, let the group decide on the best alternative. Having helped in the process, everyone will be more committed to making the solution work.

When you have made your choice, put your energy into making it succeed. Don't waste it agonizing over whether it's the best (perfect) one. No one can know what the future holds, and every decision will have drawbacks. Besides, most often if you see that your decision isn't working out, you can change it. Be content knowing you made the best choice you could and making that choice will almost certainly be better than doing nothing at all.

After her brainstorming session was completed, Marsha decided the best alternative for her was to move nearby and share the apartment of a girlfriend. This was affordable and put her far enough away from her mother for privacy and close enough for her to be of assistance in an emergency. Marsha's mother complained bitterly about being "abandoned," but soon she adapted. In fact, she soon took Marsha's suggestion developed during brainstorming and got herself a roommate of her own!

Decide How To Implement The Plan

Problem solving is really goal setting, since the plan you arrive at will be a goal. In order to achieve that goal, you will want to get specific. Work out do-able steps that will take you from where you are to where you want to go. Some goals, like Marsha's goal to leave her mother's house, don't require much planning. Others, like Sally's goal of having a day-care service, may take pages of plans. Write down your plan, so you will be certain of it. If it is a goal over which you have control, plan specific dates by which time sections of it will be completed. In that way, you can coordinate your activities so as to achieve those sections.

If you and others are working on a solution together, divide up the steps, or parts of the steps, among yourselves. Decide by what time you will each have your part of the plan completed. Commit yourself — and if you are working with others, ask them to commit themselves — to working on the plan and achieving the goal. In most cases, the first four steps will be accomplished in one session. Whether you are alone or in a group, before you conclude this session, decide on a date for a follow-up to see how the plan is working. This will make it clear that you are serious about accomplishing your goal and plan to do what is necessary.

Carry Out The Plan

Now that you have figured out what the problem is, brainstormed possible solutions, selected the best alternative, and decided how to implement the plan, the time has come for action. A great many people take all the preliminary steps and then do nothing. Don't you be one of them. The only way you can make real changes in your life is by taking action. Thinking and talking about action won't change a thing. Act early and achieve your goal while you're still enthusiastic. If you don't act early and then see your deadline approaching, carry out your goal right away. If you miss a deadline, what should you do? Forgive yourself and simply carry out your goal.

If you find that even after you work out a plan that makes sense to you, you are still unable to take action, that means that the block that exists is emotional and not in your real world. The emotional world is every bit as powerful and often more powerful than the real world. Questions such as "Am I worth acting on my own behalf?" or "Will I be punished for being self-centered?" raise issues that you may need to work on with a professional.

Another option is to decide you *are* worth it and that sometimes being selfish is a good idea. Then, even though you don't feel it, take the action step. Recognize that the anxiety you feel has to do with the fact that you are going against an early conditioning but that you *will* adjust.

If you need others to help you carry out the solution, it is likely they will do their share, especially if they had a role in deciding upon the plan. Sometimes that won't happen. People you are counting on will find themselves squeezed for time, their schedules jammed with other priorities that need attending. When others don't do as they promised, deliver a *direct assertion*. (We will discuss direct assertion in Chapter 7.) When they respond, reply using *active assertion*.

Hold A Follow-Up Meeting

If the problem involves others, anywhere from a week to a month after the initial problem-solving meeting, hold a follow-up meeting to see how the plan is going. Whether by yourself or with others, spend some time thinking about the progress or lack of progress you have made in solving your problem and meeting your goal. If your plan is working well, use this time to celebrate your accomplishment. If it is not working well, use the time to understand why and to plan and commit to alternate solutions.

Two weeks after moving out, Marsha held her follow-up meeting. She praised herself for making the move and thought about how much more peaceful her life was now. Still, she missed her mother and the warmth that was occasionally part of their relationship. She decided to phone or visit her once a week and see if that met her need to maintain contact with her.

————————————◻◼◻————————————

EXERCISE: Pretend you are Lauren in the third example at the beginning of this chapter. Using the problem-solving formula, work out a program for her to solve her problem.

EXERCISE: Pick out one of your own problems. Use the problem-solving formula to work through that problem.

The formula presented in this chapter will help you to resolve many of your personal and professional problems. It can also be useful in resolving problems with those who are willing to sit down and go through the seven steps with you. For others — or when the action is moving too fast to go through the steps — it is appropriate for you to ask for changes of behavior using the formula in the following chapter.

7

Asking Others To Change Their Behavior

Beverly was watching "Entertainment Tonight" when her friend Charles sat down to join her. After a few minutes, he reached for the remote control switch and turned on "Championship Wrestling." Beverly sat there, fuming. Finally, she exploded. *"You have some nerve,"* she screamed, *"coming over here and just doing whatever you like!"* Charles shook his head and apologized, uncertain as to why Beverly was so upset.

Sandra asked her roommate Jan to pick up a lamp she had ordered on her way home. Being an adult child, Sandra had found it hard to ask in the first place. When Jan showed up empty-handed, explaining she had forgotten to make the stop, Sandra became enraged.

Alex's neighbors played their TV loudly almost every night. He hoped they would quiet down or move away, but they never did. He became so upset that he took to coming home after they had gone to bed. Alex used to exchange friendly hellos with his neighbors, but then he took to ignoring them or even glaring at them.

As a child, you had needs that were often neglected and your rights were often violated. As an adult child, you may be seething as you wait passively for others to meet your needs or respect your rights. Or you may be lashing out aggressively. Both responses are counterproductive. Being passive seldom produces positive results. It causes you to build up tension, develop physical problems, and perhaps eventually to explode. Being aggressive can damage your relationships and provoke counterattacks. The following, then, is a constructive assertive alternative.

Determine If The Problem Is Really Yours

Use the guidelines given in Chapter 6 to determine if the problem is indeed yours. If it is yours, ask yourself what the problem is and exactly what change of behavior by the other person would resolve it. Then, using the formula outlined later in this chapter, work out your request. Think out — even write out — what you will say. If you feel particularly nervous, take the time to visualize yourself successfully asking for change. You might also practice rehearsing the situation with a friend. Having prepared yourself, you are ready for the next step, to tell others, "I have a problem." Stating that it is your problem will likely make them far less defensive and far more open to helping you get your needs and desires satisfied.

Ask If This Is A Good Time To State Your Gripe

If your complaint is small, you may want to skip this step. If you do, it is equally appropriate for others, who may be tired or involved in some other activity, to say, "Let's sit down in an hour to talk about it." To ask for time to discuss your problem, simply say, "I've got something on my mind and I'd like us to talk it out. Is now a good time?" If you are told this is not a good time, don't just walk away. Ask, "When would be a good time?" and make a definite alternate appointment. You may want to ask for a specific amount of time to discuss your problem. This will ensure you a hearing and will make it difficult for the other person to ask to be excused because of another appointment. Be certain, however, that if you ask for a definite amount of time, you limit the discussion to that time or less.

Deliver Your Assertive Message

State your problem using the "When . . . then" format. Objectively describe the problem behavior, using the word "When." "I have a problem when . . ."

"When you switched from my show to wrestling without asking . . ."

"When you didn't bring home the lamp . . ."

"When you have the TV on this loud . . ."

Bring up just one topic at a time. Bringing up two or more gripes is likely to result in the other person feeling defensive, perhaps even overwhelmed. Focus on the present or the recent past; the other person can't do a thing about your old gripes. Focus on the *behavior*, not on *the person as a whole*. Others will resist — sometimes fiercely — your attaching labels like "stupid" or "fool" to them. Instead, confine your remarks to their behavior, describing exactly what they are doing that you don't like. Make certain your remarks are phrased objectively. Avoid assumptions about the other person's motives like these:

"When you tried to get me mad at you . . ."

"When you deliberately came home without the lamp . . ."

"When you try to drive me crazy by . . ."

Assertive messages that contain assumptions seldom achieve their goals. Other people will frequently become so incensed when you tell them why they acted the way they did that they will begin arguing with you about your inference and never even give a thought to your problem.

Nan: One time I went swimming without taking my house keys. My husband locked up our apartment and left to go to the gym. When I returned, I found myself locked out and having to go to the apartment office to get a key. Trying to use the "When . . . then" formula, I said, "When you deliberately locked me out . . ." And he started yelling, "I did *not* do it 'deliberately.' If you feel I did, you should divorce me!" On and on he went. I apologized and it was maybe half an hour more before we were able to work on my problem.

After you have completed the "When" portion of the "When . . . then" formula, tell the other person the consequences of the behavior and perhaps how you feel about them.

"I have a problem. When you switched from my show to wrestling, I didn't get to finish watching my program, and I feel upset."

"I have a problem. When you didn't bring home the lamp, I wasn't able to give it as a birthday present last night, and I feel angry."

"I have a problem. When you have the TV on so loud, I can't read or relax in my home."

Once again, resist the temptation to state your inferences about someone's intention instead of your feelings:

". . . and I feel that you don't respect me."

". . . and I feel that you wanted to get back at me."

". . . and I feel that you enjoy driving me crazy."

The crucial phrase here is "I feel that." If you leave those words out, you aren't telling someone else how you feel; you're telling him how he feels.

If you are in an ongoing relationship with the other person, ask him or her to listen carefully and then recall the essence of what you have said, so you'll be certain your message got across. You might simply ask, "What did you hear me say?" Perhaps without knowing it, in this way they'll be learning to use active listening. If their active listening was accurate, say so. If it wasn't, clarify it. Active listening tends to slow down the interchange and make it more likely the other person will take the time to think about what you have said before responding.

Whether you use active listening or not, after you have delivered your assertive message, pause, and give the other person time to think about what you have said, to suggest a solution that may meet your needs. Many adult children, in a hurry to resolve the issue, rush in with a request for change. But the resolution is likely to be stronger if both you and the other person have played a hand in developing it.

Most often, when you use the "When . . . then" formula, people will make an effort to suit your needs. When that doesn't happen, deliver a *direct assertion*, a statement that tells the other person exactly what change of behavior you want.

"Please ask me if I mind before switching the channel next time."

"Please don't promise me anything you aren't sure you can do."

"Please lower the volume of your TV."

Come To A Conclusion

Once the other person has received your message, he or she may accept or reject it outright, or the other person may propose a compromise solution. If you work out a compromise, be certain you don't lose sight of the need or desire you wanted to have respected. If the problem is complex or a good solution difficult to arrive at, the two of you may want to use the problem-solving formula outlined in Chapter 6.

When the two of you have arrived at a conclusion, use active listening so both of you will be certain of what you have decided. If it is an especially important agreement, write it out and give a copy to the other person. If you live together, post the agreement on the refrigerator, so both of you will be reminded of it now and again.

At the end of your talk, arrange a time to get together and discuss how the resolution is working. You may find that the plan needs to be fine-tuned. Or you may need to replace it altogether. You may find that one of you has not been living up to his or her end of the agreement. Chances are that, by arranging for a follow-up meeting, the two of you will take the agreement more seriously and will make greater efforts to carry it out.

If You Start To Panic

Marjorie: Last night, I was determined to tell my husband how I felt about his flirting with other women. As soon as I opened my mouth, I began to feel panicky and switched on the TV, saying we would discuss it later. The panicky feeling left, but I never got started.

Adult children sometimes start to panic when they bring up difficult issues. Getting rid of the panic then becomes the issue of greatest consequence, and they quickly back away from all other issues.

Recognize that you are moving into uncharted territory, and it makes a lot of sense to be fearful of the unknown. If that is where your panicky feelings come from, just take a few deep breaths and push ahead.

For many it has to do with being overwhelmed by ghosts of the past. What is really going on in the present is lost when the past and the fear that what happened then will repeat itself takes over. The present is lost to the past, and the rational world takes second place to the emotional world. The "what ifs" take over:

- What if I'm ignored?
- What if I'm rejected?
- What if I get yelled at?
- What if I get beaten?
- What if she gets upset and I have to fix her as well?
- What if he takes it out on the kids?

These "what ifs" are grounded in your childhood. The next step is to ask yourself, "Is my fear realistic in the present?" If the answer is no, take steps to relax and gain courage, such as:

1. Talk to a friend who is supportive.
2. Talk to yourself in the mirror.
3. Use a relaxation technique.

4. Acknowledge to yourself that your fear does not exist in the present and remind yourself who you are really dealing with.
5. Recognize that others only have the power that you give them.
6. If the first five steps don't work, then work with a professional to sort things out so that you can proceed.

If the answer is yes, then you have a new set of questions. The first one is, "Is furthering communications with this person important to my life?" If the answer is no, make another choice. If the answer is yes, then examine the "what if" outcomes further.

- Can you adjust to being ignored, yelled at or rejected?
- Can you prevent any outburst toward you or the children?
- Can you let that person deal with his/her own reaction if it is totally unresponsive to you?

It is important to be able to answer yes to these questions. If you cannot, then work toward that goal with support. The sincere attempt to improve communication will be of benefit to you regardless of the reception because you will then be able to separate the reality from the fantasy and the present from the past.

Many people are pleasantly surprised when they learn one of the reasons for the difficulty has been that the other person doesn't have these skills either, and he or she will respond differently when they learn what the possibilities are.

8

Handling Criticism

The last chapter taught you how to ask constructively for change. This chapter will teach you how to respond constructively to criticism and requests for change from others.

Marsha could tell something was wrong by the way her husband Gary pursed his lips and avoided making eye contact. She nervously steered clear of him as he read the paper, but as she was serving dinner, the anger she feared burst forth. "TV dinners *again!*" he said. "Can't you fix something decent once in a while? Clothes all over the house, shoes in the middle of the floor, dirty cups every-where . . . Would it kill you to spend five minutes cleaning up the place?" Marsha wanted to ask Gary to share in the housework since they both had full-time jobs. But all such thoughts were forgotten as Gary's anger poured forth.

"He doesn't love me anymore," she told herself. "He's going to divorce me and I'll be all alone." She panicked. Her body froze stiff and a wave of anxiety spread over her. She wanted to cry out, "Don't leave me!" but instead she just cried.

Like Marsha, you tend to panic in the face of criticism from others — and the anger that often accompanies it. Criticism to you means that you are not loved and will soon be left. You may want to respond to the criticism, but your fear of abandonment tends to be so strong it overrides your other goals. So you cry, you change the subject, you become submissive, you become seductive, you run away. The issue that provoked the anger remains, but for the moment, the panic is gone.

This chapter will give you some ideas on how to deal with panic. And, with your anxiety reduced, it will teach you skills for handling criticism constructively.

Ask For Reassurance

Ask those who are close to you to reassure you, before they give you criticism, that they love you and will not abandon you. Marsha, for example, told Gary, "I have a problem. When you criticize me, I start thinking you don't love me anymore and that you're going to leave me — and I panic. From now on, when you criticize me, will you please reassure me that you still love me and will stay with me. Maybe then I won't panic and cry. And maybe then I'll be able to deal with your criticism."

Call "Time Out"

If you are feeling panicky or are not sure how to respond to criticism, call "time out." Simply say, "I'd like to think about what you've had to say. I'll get back to you in an hour [tonight, tomorrow]." This way you will have time to think about the criticism and to formulate and rehearse your response. The other person will generally react positively when you call "time out" as it signals that you are giving serious consideration to the criticism.

Request Specifics

When adult children are criticized, they often ignore or downplay the criticism, hoping it will simply go away. At the same time it reinforces their idea that they are worthless and that their character flaws have been discovered. The problem itself gets lost and only serves to confirm their negative sense of self. But the reality is that the problem does exist and, like dirt pushed under a rug, it won't go away. It gathers, it festers, it grows. Yesterday's dirt joins with today's dirt, and before long you have a huge lump under the carpet. It is wiser by far to deal with the dirt, to deal with the criticism as it comes up, to understand it, to work on it, and to let it go.

When you don't understand criticism, the first step in dealing with it constructively is to request specifics. Doing so requires simply that you get others to focus on exactly what they don't like. Most often, this will come down to things you *did* or *said*. For example:

> *Lynn:* You don't love me anymore.
> *Bill:* What have I *done* that leads you to say that?
> *Lynn:* You didn't call to wish me a happy birthday.

> *Sarah:* You embarrassed me.
> *Jim:* What did I *do* or *say* that embarrassed you?
> *Sarah:* Telling that joke about my losing the parrot in front of my friends.

> *Janice:* You should be ashamed of yourself.
> *Derrick:* What did I *do* that I should be ashamed of?
> *Janice:* Talking to George while I was left standing here all alone!

Requesting specifics can also be useful in helping your critics to understand their own system of right and wrong. For example:

"You shouldn't go to ACoA meetings so often."

"What is it about my attending ACoA meetings that you feel is wrong?"

Said in a nondefensive way, this will encourage your critics to expand on their thinking. They may tell you that, in their opinion, ACoA meetings are a waste of time, that you're too busy already, that you should have resolved your issues already. In such cases, your critics will have the opportunity to examine their own right/wrong structure and will be encouraged to be more assertive and direct with you in the future.

Frequently when you request specifics you will uncover a hidden issue underneath the surface. Your critics will respond with revealing answers, such as, "I don't like you going to ACoA meetings so much because then I don't get to see you as much as I'd like," or "Those people mean more to you than I do."

Guess Specifics

Sometimes when you ask your critics for specifics, they won't be able to give you some or all of them. In such cases, you can guess specifics. This may lead to their acknowledging that one of your guesses is correct. Or it may encourage them to come up with their own specifics. For example:

John: I don't like the way you treated my mother.
Rita: What exactly did I do? (Requesting specifics.)
John: Well, you weren't very nice to her.
Rita: Was it my not laughing at her joke? (Guessing specifics.)
John: No, it wasn't that.
Rita: Was it my not offering her seconds at dinner? (Guessing specifics.)
John: No, although I suppose you could have done that.
Rita: Was it my telling her we're too busy to come to her place for dinner next Friday? (Guessing specifics.)
John: Well, you know, she gets lonely all by herself.

Ask For Additional Complaints

Once you succeed in getting the other person to be specific, you may want to ask for additional complaints. If you're typical, faced with such a suggestion, you'll say to yourself, "Why would I do that? Don't I have enough problems with the original criticism?" The reason to ask for additional complaints is that doing so brings all the problems out into the open, where you can work on them. Remember, you're okay no matter what the criticism, and since the problems are no secret to the other person, why shouldn't you know too? To ask for additional complaints, once you have finished requesting specifics and guessing specifics and have received a reply, simply say, "Is there anything else?" For example:

Jules: You don't care about me.
Donna: What have I done that leads you to say that? (Requesting specifics.)
Jules: You showed up 20 minutes late for our date.
Donna: Is there anything else? (Asking for additional complaints.)
Jules: This isn't the first time. You've been late the last few times.
Donna: Okay, anything else? (Asking for additional complaints.)
Jules: You didn't ask me how my cold is doing.
Donna: Okay, anything else? (Asking for additional complaints.)
Jules: No, that's about it.

Use Active Listening

Another way to get your critics to explain their objections is to use the skill of active listening. Even after you have uncovered all objections, you may want to use active listening as it helps to defuse your critics' emotions. Most of what people want when they criticize you is to be heard, and when you use active listening, your critics will have no doubt they have been heard. For example:

Toni: I'm mad at you.
Art: What did I do? (Requesting specifics.)
Toni: Selling our car for $1,700. You broke our agreement.
Art: Sounds like you're really upset. (Active listening.)
Toni: Yes I am. You promised not to take anything under $2,000.
Art: You feel like I gave the car away. (Active listening.)
Toni: Right. Couldn't you have said, "No, I'll wait for another offer?" Couldn't you have just said, "No?"
Art: You think I should have turned him down. (Active listening.)

Toni: Yeah, the $300 we didn't get . . . there are a lot of things we could have done with $300.
Art: We could have used that money. (Active listening.)
Toni: Right.

Agree With The Truth

Criticism you are given will often be true. Your critic says you are late — and you are. Your critic says you made a mess — and you did. Your critic says you look nervous — and you are. When criticism is true, your best response is to agree with it. If the relationship is valuable to you, then be responsive to the other person's feelings. And if you plan on doing anything about the criticism, add that too. Consider these responses:

"You're late."
"That's true. I feel bad if it upset you, and I'll work on doing better."

"You forgot to prepare your report."
"You're right. I'm sorry if you were inconvenienced. I'll have it ready by two."

"You haven't said a thing all night."
"You're right. I hope you don't feel ignored, but I don't feel talkative."

Agree With The Odds

Sometimes, it's a question of possibilities. Your critics will say that if you don't do as they suggest, things won't go well. You can certainly agree that it's at least possible that they're right. You can agree with the odds and still, if you choose, reject the changes they suggest. For example:

Chet: If you don't wear a jacket, you'll catch cold.
Steve: I appreciate your concern and you may be right, but I enjoy the light feeling I get from going outside without my jacket on.

Ellen: If you leave Barnie, you'll probably never find another man.

Joan: Men certainly are hard to come by nowadays, so you might well turn out to be right. But I've had enough of Barnie's abusive behavior, so I'm leaving.

Sarah: If you get a motorcycle, you're likely to get into an accident.

Todd: I appreciate your concern for my safety, and you're right — a lot of motorcyclists do have accidents. And I might be just one more. But I find motorcycling very exciting.

Disagree With The Criticism

When you are criticized, you have the right to disagree. All you need to do is say, "I disagree" and then state your reasons. If you adopt an "I'm okay — You're okay" attitude about the disagreement, chances are the other person will also. Follow the rules of conduct in Chapter 10 to keep your discussion on track. If, in your opinion, the criticism you are given is extreme or abusive, use the skills in Chapter 9 to defend your boundaries.

A skill you may find useful in disagreeing is agreement with your critic's right to differ. Using this skill, you agree that your critic has a valid opinion, although you don't accept it or intend to change your behavior. Beginning your reply with "I can see how you might think . . ." makes it easy for you to then fill in the criticism and a reason your critic might be right. For example:

Tami: How can you work as a waitress? With your education, you could do much better.
Nan: I can see how you might think I could do better. After all, I do have a Master's in Art. But I enjoy the people I meet on my job, the hours are short and the money is great. So I'm going to stick with it for now.

David: I think you've gone to enough 12-Step meetings. I mean, haven't you heard everything there is to hear?
Eileen: I can see how you might think that. I've been going for a long time and I certainly have learned a lot. But there's always something new to pick up. Besides, I don't go to learn anything. I go to keep my life on track.

Ann-Marie: I don't think you should buy a house now. Prices are so ridiculously high, they're bound to fall soon.

Kim: I can see how you might think that this isn't a good time to buy. After all, prices have gone up 17 percent this year. But I think they're going to go still higher.

Notice how each of the responses made the criticism seem reasonable. Some even contained evidence to support the criticism. No one was made to be "right" or "wrong." When you agree with your critic's right to differ, the two of you emerge simply as well-meaning, intelligent people who have differing opinions.

Bringing Your Skills Together

Dialogue One

Danny: You're not such a good mommy.

Mom: What did I do that you don't like? (Requests specifics.)

Danny: You know.

Mom: Is it that I forgot to come back to tuck you in last night? (Guesses specifics.)

Danny: No.

Mom: Is it because I was late picking you up from Cub Scouts last week? (Guesses specifics.)

Danny: No.

Mom: Is it because I haven't bought you the remote control car I promised you? (Guesses specifics.)

Danny: You promised a week ago.

Mom: You feel like I've taken long enough and I should get it already. (Active listening.)

Danny: Yeah!

Mom: I agree that it *is* long enough, and I'll go to the store tomorrow. Okay? (Agrees with the truth.)

Danny: Okay.

Mom: Is there anything else I've done that you don't like? (Asks for additional complaints.)

Danny: No, that's all.

Dialogue Two

Mort: I don't want you going back to school.

Samantha: What is it about my going back to school that you don't like? (Requests specifics.)

Mort: I don't know, it's just that it'll take lots of time.

Samantha: Yes, it will take a lot of time. What is it about my taking a lot of time that you don't like? (Agrees with the truth and requests specifics.)

Mort: I don't know.

Samantha: Is it maybe that I won't have as much time for *you?* (Guesses specifics.)

Mort: Well, that's a possibility.

Samantha: I agree. I probably won't have as much. But I'll be sure to make time for my man. Anything else? (Agrees with the truth and requests specifics.)

Mort: Well, it'll cost a lot of money.

Samantha: That's true. But I'll make far more my first year as a teacher. (Agrees with the truth.)

Mort: I just wonder if you're really committed.

Samantha: (Active listening.) You think I won't finish or won't really take a job if I do.

Mort: Well, you never did use your hairstylist's license.

Samantha: That's true. (Agrees with the truth.)

Mort: And lots of women who study education don't end up teaching.

Samantha: I agree. Lots of women do drop out or don't use their education, and I can see how you might think I'll do the same. But I *will* finish and I *will* become a teacher. Is there anything else? (Agrees with the odds and requests specifics.)

Mort: Even if you do succeed, there's so darn much competition out there . . .

Samantha: I can understand your thinking. There *used* to be too many teachers, but now there are too few — and especially among Spanish teachers. Anything else? (Agrees with the critic's right to differ.)

Mort: Just one thing. I just hope those students are gonna know how lucky they are!

This chapter has taught you how to respond to criticism constructively. Sometimes people will go beyond criticism and will try to force you to give in. How to defend yourself is among the subjects of our next chapter.

9

Establishing And Defending Boundaries

I'm a pushover. My son wants a babysitter, he comes over and drops the kid off. Doesn't even call first anymore. My other son gets in debt, he calls to beg me for money. Now he's moved back home. Imagine, a 32-year-old living with his mother! My neighbor comes by most every morning, talks my ear off while I serve her coffee. Now she's after me to lend her some of my clothes.

— *Marcia*

I put in my 9 to 5 repairing computers, and then I'm ready to go home. But half the time my boss has a last-minute job for me. And then there are "emergency" jobs that sometimes last into the night, sometimes all weekend. As a result of this, I'm out of tune with my wife, a stranger to my children. My mother came from Korea last month, and I asked for the week off to show her around, to spend time with her. But the answer was no. My boss said he couldn't spare me.

— *Warren*

I thought my problems were over when I got a divorce. But my new husband, he's turning out just like the old one! He's drinking more and more, yelling and hitting — things he never did at first. If only he'd be the way he was at first, I think we could have a nice loving home.

— *Nikki*

A boundary is a *barrier* between you and other people, a limitation beyond which you will not go and beyond which others are not welcome. Adult children like Marcia, Warren, Nikki, and you typically have difficulty establishing and defending boundaries. You grew up in a family in which boundaries were blurred or nonexistent. If you were sexually abused, even your body's boundaries were not respected. Consequently you aren't sure what boundaries are appropriate for you, how to establish those boundaries with other people, and how to defend those boundaries against attack.

How To Know When You Need Boundaries

There are five ways of knowing when you need boundaries. First, you need boundaries in situations in which you feel any of the following:

- Beaten down;
- Angry;
- Depressed;
- Violated;
- Used;
- Overworked.

If you are well connected with your feelings, these warning signs should adequately alert you to situations in which you need boundaries. Marcia and Warren, for example, feel used. Nikki feels angry. These are good signs that they need to establish boundaries with the people in their lives.

If you are not well in touch with your feelings, examine your relationships in terms of whether others are giving you a *fair exchange*. People exchange cash, goods, services and sentiments. Out of a misplaced sense of loyalty, adult children often give and give and give, even when they're not getting. Quite often they fool themselves into believing they are getting because they enjoy giving. They are not the same. Be loyal to others, but be loyal to yourself first. Be loyal to others, but set reasonable limits to your loyalty. If the rewards of a personal or business relationship don't match the costs, you need to renegotiate the terms of the relationship.

To examine any of your personal or business relationships, take a piece of paper and draw a line down the middle. On the left side, put COST and on the right side put REWARD. Fill out the sheet and then look it over, asking yourself, "Am I getting to about the same degree that I'm giving?" When Warren did this, he found that he was giving 80 hours a week, sacrificing his relationship with his wife, children and mother, and jeopardizing his health. Viewing his business relationship this way, Warren could easily see that he was not getting a fair exchange and needed to renegotiate the terms of his job.

Another way of checking to see if you need boundaries is to look at what other people are doing. Do your neighbors have their older children dropping children off unannounced? Are they having their older children move back home? Do they work 80 hours a week? Consider looking at your job description to see if it calls for the things that are being asked of you.

Get the opinion of someone whose judgment you value. Make sure it's someone who is not profiting directly from your efforts. (Warren, for example, should not ask his boss if he should continue to work 80-hour weeks.) Adult children are often so isolated they don't know what is typical.

Ask yourself: "If someone I love came to me and described this situation, what would my advice be?" Your answer might well be to stop taking it, to say no, to set up boundaries, to defend your boundaries. If that is your advice for another person, shouldn't *you* follow it as well?

Setting Personal Boundaries

Boundaries can be decided upon before or during the time when they are needed. They can also be changed. The ideal time to decide upon boundaries is in advance of their being needed. When you plan in advance, you have plenty of time to think through what boundaries you want and to prepare what you'll say if someone tries to cross them. Examples of boundaries include:

- I won't allow alcohol, cigarettes, or other drugs in my home.
- I won't allow anyone to hit me or to verbally abuse me.
- I won't lend money or my car to anyone except family members.
- I won't work Sundays.

Boundaries in dating situations are often best decided upon in advance and brought forth when they are needed. Diane, for example, is a newly divorced woman who didn't want to get involved quickly with anyone. When George asked her out, she told him she didn't feel ready to date anyone yet, but that if he'd like her to go with him to a party or a dance, or if he would arrange for them to join another couple, that would be fine. At the end of the evening, when he asked to come in, she told him she'd be open to having him come in for coffee the next time they got together.

Many single people say it's especially difficult putting the brakes on physical intimacy. If you have decided on your boundaries beforehand, you will find this considerably easier. When George kissed Diane the second time they went out, she told him, "I can tell now that you like me and want to get closer. I'm not ready right now, but when I am ready, I'll let you know."

Boundaries can also be set on the spot, during a situation. Even though you haven't thought the situation through in advance, and perhaps even though you don't have a good reason, you can still announce a boundary, just because you say so. A student named Elliot, for example, was once helping a friend move when the friend said it was time to take the refrigerator down the stairs. Elliot had never considered the situation before and had no boundaries in place. Still, he recalled that his father had once hurt his back while moving a stove, so Elliot announced, "No, not me. That's too heavy for me." His friend shrugged his shoulders and told Elliot, "Okay, then I'll have someone else do it tomorrow."

Changing Personal Boundaries

You are not bound to abide forever by previously set boundaries. You can change your mind just because you want to. It is often best to announce changes before those boundaries are needed. Marcia, for example, might well want to tell her son that, in the future, he needs to call her first to see if she's free and would like to babysit. She might announce that her other son is welcome to continue living with her — but only for the next three months. Warren could announce to his boss that, beginning the following month, he'll no longer be available to work on weekends. Nikki could announce to her husband that she will leave if he ever hits her again.

Negotiating Boundaries

Marie: I have only been married three months and I think the marriage is in trouble already. Every Sunday like clockwork, my in-laws drop by and stay through dinner. I could scream, but I keep my mouth shut because I don't want to cause problems. I finally told my husband how I felt and he said I was being selfish.

Sometimes it will be important for you and another person (or even several others) to jointly agree on boundaries you will have in your relationships with other people:

Must the in-laws call in advance? Will guests be allowed to smoke? May a friend stay with you for a month? By agreeing beforehand, the two of you can prevent conflicts among yourselves while presenting a united front and a stronger hand to others.

In other cases, you will want to negotiate boundaries to use with each other: How far can displays of affection go in public? In private? Who decides what TV shows to watch? Should you combine your money or have separate accounts? Under what circumstances can one of you spend a substantial sum? In negotiating a boundary with another, use the following steps:

1. Define what is acceptable to you, what boundary you want.
2. Express your thoughts and feelings about the problem and propose your boundary to the other person.
3. Listen to the other person express his thoughts and feelings about the problem and let him propose the boundary he thinks best.
4. Work out an accommodation.

If the problem is emotionally charged or important, you may want to use active listening to make sure the messages sent are the messages received. If the problem is complex, you may wish to use the problem-solving formula outlined in Chapter 6.

Usually people working together in good faith can find an accommodation: "We'll tell my folks they're welcome to drop by unannounced only the first Sunday of every month." "We'll flip a coin to decide which show to watch and we'll tape the other one." "Either of us can spend up to $500 without getting an okay from the other."

When the two of you cannot work out a compromise acceptable to both of you, you may want to seek professional help while meanwhile setting up a personal boundary for yourself. For example, if Marie could not negotiate boundaries with her husband, she might arrange to be out of the house Sundays while waiting to see a counselor.

Defending Boundaries

Whether announced in advance, announced when a situation arises, changed, or even negotiated, your boundaries will frequently be tested. Some people won't take you seriously. They'll try to get you to give your boundaries up, to adopt boundaries that are "fairer" — to them. They'll try to wear you down by giving you lots of reasons why you "should" give up your boundaries. They'll try to make you feel guilty and to drop your boundaries so they can go back to using you. Because you are not used to having boundaries, you may well find it difficult to counter their efforts.

Fortunately, there are skills you can use to defend your boundaries. Using these skills, you can outlast even the most persistent person.

Call "Time Out"

When your boundaries are challenged and you're not sure how to respond, call "time out." This will give you plenty of time to calm down, to practice saying "No," and to prepare possible counteroffers. For example, the next time Marcia's son asked her for money, she wasn't ready to respond. So she told him, "Let me think about it. I'll get back to you tomorrow." This gave her plenty of time to calmly prepare her response and to rehearse it with a friend.

When Joan's father called to invite her to a family dinner being given for a visiting aunt, she wasn't sure she wanted to come. Joan didn't like the way this aunt always asked embarrassing personal questions of her in front of everyone. Rather than follow her usual routine and agree to attend, Joan called "time out." "I'll look at my schedule and get back to you," she told her father. This gave Joan the luxury of having time to get in touch with her feelings. Joan had recently been divorced and she squirmed at the thought of being grilled for details. She called her father and told him she'd be unable to attend.

Deliver An Assertive "No!"

As an adult child, you have a near-perfect record of saying "Yes." It may be difficult for you to say "No," but if you are to defend your boundaries, it is important that you learn. If you just say "I'm not sure" or "I'd rather not," you're conveying a weak conviction, and others may well try to break through your boundaries. But the word "No" is definite. It lets others know you will not allow your boundaries to be breached.

An assertive, definite "No" or "No thanks" is the best kind. When you say "No" as though you really mean it, others are less likely to try to get you to change your mind. To deliver an assertive "No":

- Stand up straight;
- Look the other person in the eyes;
- Speak clearly and firmly.

EXERCISE: Practice saying "No" to a friend, into a tape recorder, while looking at a mirror. This is especially important if you are a woman, as women's "Nos" are often not accepted at face value by men.

If the request seems especially important or emotionally charged, you may want to use active listening before delivering your "No." This will let the other person know you have heard the request, know it's important, but you can't agree to it. For example: "You'd like me to help you pick out a new car tomorrow. I wish I had time, but I'm busy all this week."

After delivering your "No," you may choose to propose an alternative. Joan, for example, invited her parents over for dinner a week later — several days *after* her aunt would be gone.

Start wherever you are. If you have difficulty saying "No," begin by imagining doing it in unimportant circumstances. Then, try it out in those same circumstances. When a caller asks if you're free, say, "No, please call back in 10 minutes." When a lady at the supermarket offers you samples, say "No, thanks." When a bank teller asks if you'd like 20s, say "No, thanks, I'd prefer 10s." Gradually, move from saying "No" to strangers to saying "No" to acquaintances and friends.

> *Joyce:* I remember the first time I practiced saying "No." A neighbor asked to borrow my car. I took a deep breath and said, "No, I never lend my car. But if you'd like, you can call a cab from here." I didn't know what to expect. Would he yell at me? Would he never talk to me again? In reality, all he did was say, "No problem" and walked off. Instead of rejecting me, he seems to treat me with more respect since then.

Broken Record

People will occasionally try to get you to give up your boundaries by asking you over and over again, by giving you lots of reasons why you should, and by criticizing you for refusing. They hope to wear you down to the point where you'll let them have their way. The broken record technique is the perfect skill to use with people who won't take "No" for an answer. Using it, you'll be able to defend your boundaries against even the most persistent attack. To use broken record, all you do is repeat your refusal statement over and over again, just like a broken record. Speak in a calm, relaxed tone. Hold your statement to one short sentence, and use the same words, the same tone of voice, each time. Many people let themselves be talked out of their boundaries because they feel they have to give a new reason each time they are asked, but you don't. You can just give the same reason over and over and over again, no matter what issues the other person raises. When you have delivered your message, stop, be silent. Let the situation become a little awkward for the other person. You win if you use broken record one time more than your manipulator makes a request.

If you're just getting started, you may want to find a friend and practice saying nothing more than the word "No" over and over in response to whatever your friend asks. Remember to stand up straight, look the other person in the eye and say your "No" clearly and firmly. Here's how one practice session went:

> *Rick:* Marla, I'm flying out of town tomorrow afternoon. Will you take me to the airport?
> *Marla:* No.
> *Rick:* But I'd be so happy to have you there to see me off.
> *Marla:* No.
> *Rick:* Look, it'd only take an hour of your time.
> *Marla:* No.
> *Rick:* If gas is a problem, I'll pay your gas.
> *Marla:* No.
> *Rick:* I'll fill up your whole tank.
> *Marla:* No.
> *Rick:* Why won't you take me?
> *Marla:* No.
> *Rick:* Remember when you needed a ride to the garage? *I* was there for *you*. Now *I* need help.
> *Marla:* No.
> *Rick:* Look, I'll owe you one. Whenever you need a favor, ask and I promise it's yours.
> *Marla:* No.
> *Rick:* Marla, isn't this what friends are for? To help each other out?
> *Marla:* No.
> *Rick:* If you don't come across, I'm going to have to take a taxi, and that's expensive.
> *Marla:* No.

This exercise will help desensitize you and so make it easier for you to say "No" in real-life situations. It will also make it clear to you that you don't *have* to respond to others' manipulative efforts, that you don't *have* to answer others' every question. You can "Just Say No!"

Broken record is most effectively used together with the skills for handling criticism you learned in the last chapter. Begin by agreeing with the truth, agreeing with the odds, or agreeing with the critic's right to differ. Then, if the other person continues to attack your boundaries, go into broken record. For example, Marcia tried out this skill when her neighbor came by to borrow some clothes:

Neighbor: Marcia, I have a job interview next week and I'd like to borrow your suit — you know, that "serious" brown one.

Marcia: I'm glad you like my suit, but I don't lend my clothes.

Neighbor: But I really need a good-looking suit.

Marcia: I agree that you do, but I don't lend my clothes. [Agrees with the truth and broken record.]

Neighbor: If I wear my old suit, I won't look as good and I probably won't get the job.

Marcia: I agree that you'd be more likely to get the job wearing my suit than your old one. But I don't lend my clothes. [Agrees with the odds and broken record.]

Neighbor: Why won't you lend me your suit?

Marcia: I don't lend my clothes. [Broken record.]

Neighbor: I bet when you were little, your mom gave your brothers toys you thought were yours, and now you find it hard to share.

Marcia: I can see how you might think that. Lots of people are touched by early influences. But that never happened, and I don't lend my clothes. [Agrees with the critic's right to differ and broken record.]

Neighbor: I know you're afraid I'll tear it or dirty it. Well, I can assure you, I'd treat it like my own.

Marcia: I'm sure you would, but I don't lend my clothes. [Agrees with the truth and broken record.]

Neighbor: It doesn't look like you're going to help me out.

Marcia: You're right, I'm not. I don't lend my clothes. [Agrees with the truth and broken record.]

Note: Don't get bogged down in answering "why" questions. "Why" used in manipulative situations like the one illustrated above is not a legitimate request for information so much as it is part of a search for ammunition that can be used against you. Giving lots of excuses will typically result only in the other person trying to respond to all your excuses in order to win you over. When Marcia, for example, was asked, "Why won't you lend me your suit?" she simply repeated her broken record line. Suppose she had instead explained, "I'm afraid you'll get it dirty." That would have left the neighbor an opening to say "I'll guarantee to clean it if I get it dirty" — and very likely would have made it difficult for Marcia to continue resisting her manipulation.

Delivering "If . . . Then" Contingencies

If the other person persists in efforts to breach your boundaries, you may choose to continue agreeing and using broken record. You may choose to use the "When . . . then" formula to ask him or her to stop asking. Or, you may want to deliver an "If . . . then" contingency. Simply put, "If . . . then" contingencies tell the other person what you will do if you continue to have your boundaries violated. Keep your statements unemotional, your consequences in proportion to the behavior you want stopped. For example:

"If you keep bringing up the subject, I'll leave."

"If you keep yelling, I'll hang up."

"If you keep asking me to decide now, the answer is No."

It needn't be said like a threat — you're just saying, "If you do this, I'll do that."

One thing more, when you do use "If . . . then" contingencies, it's vital that you follow through. If you don't, your future contingencies won't be believed.

No matter how well you learn the skills in the preceding chapters for solving problems, asking others to change their behavior, handling criticism, and setting boundaries, you will occasionally have fights. The following chapter will teach you how to fight fair.

10

Fighting Fair

Helen felt like a volcano about to explode. "You humiliated me!" she screamed. "Flirting in front of everyone!"

"I was *not* flirting," her husband countered. "I was just being friendly. That's more than *you* can say, Miss Sour Puss. *You* didn't have a smile for anyone the whole night."

"Look at yourself," Helen replied, "a balding, middle-aged man pretending to be young. A married man with two daughters pretending to be single."

"When you talk like that, I wish I *were* single," he said.

"Last New Year's Eve, as the clock struck 12, you just *had* to have a dance with Debbie. Valentine's Day, you were flirting with what's-her-name from your office. No wonder women call up asking for you — you're a loose man! A tramp!"

"There was *one* call," he said, "a mistake . . . Look, I've had enough of this . . . I'm going out."

Imagine what a football game would be like if there were no rules of conduct, if everyone could hit anyone anytime in any way they chose. Players would be punching each other, pulling on each other's face masks, kneeing each other. Players would refuse to wait for the ball to be hiked before charging, refuse to stop when they ran out of bounds . . . Riots would ensue. The scene would be chaotic. Large numbers of people would be hurt or injured and no one would have fun. Goals might be scored, but at tremendous cost.

With rules, however, football games proceed in an orderly fashion. There is conflict, but it's controlled conflict. If someone oversteps his bounds, he is cited for it and penalized.

There are rules for football and hostile takeovers and even war, but most people have no rules when they fight with close friends and loved ones. You saw the chaos that can result from this when you were a child, how disagreements in your family often turned into verbal — and even physical — free-for-alls, complete with screaming and cursing and threats and beatings. You hated this as a child, but chances are as an adult you are following the same pattern. You may know no other way.

It doesn't have to be that way. Just as rules allow football games to proceed in an orderly fashion, rules can help you and others to fight fair. Here are some basic procedural rules and some *dos* and *don'ts* you and others can use next time you have a fight. Go over them together at a time when things are relatively peaceful. You may want to change some or add some to suit your particular needs or desires. For example, you may want to be able to call "time outs" if things get too intense. Regardless of what rules you agree on, make sure that you do agree to some rules. And so these rules will be taken seriously, consider posting them on a wall where you and others will be reminded of them and can refer to them.

Procedural Rules

1. Ask if this is a good time to bring up your problem. If it's not, agree on another time.
2. Express the problem briefly, including the feelings you have about the problem.
3. The other person waits for you to finish and then uses active listening to restate both the message and any feelings behind it. If the other person isn't familiar with this skill, say, "When I'm done talking, please tell me what you heard me say so I'll know you got it the way I meant it."
4. Agree that the message was accurately received, or clarify it. If you clarify it, ask the other person to once again use active listening. Continue until you agree that the message has been accurately received.
5. The other person conveys any views and feelings relevant to the subject, while you use active listening.

At times when emotions run high, people are seldom prepared to solve their problems logically. This procedure helps to dissipate those emotions by giving each of you a chance to vent them and know that you are understood. It slows down the argument and prevents it from rushing headlong in destructive directions. It encourages both parties to listen to the other and not just wait for a chance to speak.

Do

Bring up one problem at a time. It is impossible to discuss five — or even two — problems at once. Try, and you will go from topic to topic, and your discussion will become more like an indictment. Others will feel defensive and overwhelmed.

Focus on the present. People often save up gripes, as though they're putting them in a little sack. He forgets to fill up the car — but you don't say anything — you just put the gripe in the sack. He forgets your birthday, and you put it in the sack. He goes through a red light, and you put it in the sack. Then one day, he shows up 20 minutes late — and you dump the whole sack on top of his head!

Gunnysacking, as this is called, makes for excitement and good theater, but it causes havoc in your relationships. Better to speak up on things you don't like as they happen. What happened last week or last year can't be changed, but present behavior can be. Those other gripes will not automatically go away because you've eliminated them from the discussion. But, for now, they only make things more complicated and get in the way of working through the current problem.

Be specific about your complaint. Vague complaints like "You disappointed me" won't get you anywhere. Instead, be specific. Tell others just what was said and where and when.

Express your feelings. It's healthy for you to say how you feel and important for the other person to know. Until you have expressed your feelings, you may not be prepared to move on and work on a rational resolution.

Allow the other person to express himself fully. Don't interrupt.

Where possible, use the skills described in Chapters 6, 7, 8 and 9. Using the "When . . . then" formula and skills like requesting specifics and agreeing with the truth can help your fight proceed more smoothly.

Compromise. In most cases, the two of you will be able to find some middle ground you can both live with. After you have both spent your emotions, you may want to arrive at it using the problem-solving formula.

Complain when the rules are violated. If the rules are to stand, you will have to remind each other of them when they are ignored.

Don't

Don't hit.

Don't yell, swear, or use sarcasm. These behaviors only serve to upset others. They focus others' attention away from your complaint and toward the way you communicated it.

Don't label others. Calling others "dumb," "crazy," "selfish," "paranoid," or any other label will only make them defensive and ready to counterattack. Be specific instead. Tell others what they *did* that you didn't like.

Don't label others' behavior or ideas. Instead of characterizing others' behavior or ideas as "stupid," "idiotic," or with any other label, discuss them on their merits. Why was a particular behavior unfortunate? Why won't an idea work?

Don't make assumptions. People often react in a highly negative way when you tell them their motives. So don't tell them *why* they were late ("You just love to embarrass me"), *why* they didn't call ("You're still trying to get back at me because . . ."), or *why* they said what they did ("You've always hated my mother"). None of us can read minds, and many times your assumptions will turn out to be false.

Don't put the entire relationship on the line. In the heat of arguments, you may be tempted to say you're thinking of ending the relationship if you can't have your way. Don't. Doing so will cause some people to refuse automatically even to compromise in the face of threats. Others will give in but will resent you for it — a situation likely to bring about further problems later on. And people who have never given a thought to ending their relationship with you may begin to doubt whether it has a future and whether they should invest much more in it.

Of all of the concepts taught in this book, fighting fair is the one that is the hardest for most adult children to stick with. The very idea of conflict creates a great deal of anxiety for you. It brings up all your childhood fears. When there was conflict in your family, chances are you were emotionally or physically abused, or someone else was emotionally or physically abused. If you tried to intervene, you would either get hurt or be ignored. You felt invisible and powerless. It was a situation without hope. You vowed you would not live your life that way. As a result you grew up terrified of and repressing your own anger. You knew you didn't want to "be like them."

As a result, the only time you express anger is when it reaches the level of rage and cannot be contained. When that happens, it is not possible for you to fight fair because all of your energy is used to try to maintain some control over your behavior. You know that loss of control will mean that someone will get hurt or worse. The other person involved will sense the degree to which you are holding back and will become frightened as well. As a result it is hard to even hold onto what the fight is supposed to be about, let alone begin to deal with it.

The situation now, unlike when you were a child, is *not* without hope. There are a couple of things that you can do. One is to practice recognizing when you feel discomfort and attempt to address that problem at that stage, before it builds. That will take a lot of practice because it is not unusual for adult children to take hours or even days before they realize they were disturbed or angry or upset by something that happened.

The other thing you can do is acknowledge to yourself when you feel enraged that your reaction is bigger than the current problem. You may not believe it at the time, but it is. The over-reaction must be addressed first. This can be done in a variety of ways. You may decide to work out or jog or close your car windows and scream or bang a plastic bat against a wall. Pick an energy release that will work for you and stay with it until some of the energy is spent and you feel more in control. Then begin this chapter over and see if you can follow the process that has been outlined. This is very hard work, but it is crucial.

11

Ending Conversations, Ending Visits

Ending Conversations

Adult children often feel stuck in conversations, unsure of how to conclude them in a friendly manner. Here are some ideas you may find helpful.

Plead a prior commitment.

"Well, I'm due back at work now."

"Excuse me, but I have a three o'clock appointment."

"Forgive me, but I have to go pick up my daughter."

Express a preference.

"Excuse me, I'm going to go say hello to George."

"I've got to go freshen my drink. Excuse me."

"I'm going home now. It's getting late."

Thank the other person.

"Thanks for the advice, Albert. Bye."

"I appreciate your help, Sam. Bye."

Summarize your agreements.

"So you'll take a look at my proposal and call me next week."

"See you on Wednesday."

"So we'll both brainstorm and share what we come up with tomorrow."

Show interest in future contact.

"I hope to see you here again."

"Let's exchange phone numbers so we can talk more later."

Issue an invitation. Review Chapter 4 for details on asking for what you want.

Be honest when you end your conversations. Dishonesty can create ill will and can get back to you. Don't say "I'll be right back" when you don't intend to do so. The other person may well wait around for you. Don't say you have an important appointment to keep when you don't. You'd be surprised how many people have said that, only to be spotted shortly thereafter in malls, parks, and restaurants, much to their embarrassment. Don't ask for someone's phone number unless you intend to call. That person may become bitter waiting day after day for you to call. If the other person asks for your number, don't give it out unless you would welcome a call. If the other person asks to get together with you at a specific time, don't agree unless you want to. It may be easier in the short run to pretend you'd welcome future contact, but it is likely to be far more difficult in the long run. Instead say, "I'd rather leave it open." If the other person refuses to accept your decision, you can begin agreeing and using broken record, saying for example, "I agree that we have a lot in common, but I'd rather leave it open."

You can also signal that you are ready to leave with your body language. The key is to *do something different.* The following signs, with or without accompanying words, should alert others to your intent:

• Stand up;
• Fidget;

- Put your jacket on;
- Talk slower or faster;
- Give your voice a higher or a lower pitch;
- Respond less, both verbally and nonverbally;
- Move toward the door as you walk;
- Move away from the other person in circles that get larger and larger as you talk.

When you finish your statement, leave. If you continue to hang around, you will be sending a double message, and the other person may not take you seriously.

EXERCISE: With a friend, pretend that you have been talking for a while and practice ending conversations. Each time, ask your friend to tell you what you did well and how you could do even better.

Ending Visits

It is not unusual for an adult child to have difficulty ending a visit. Most of the time, you can end your visits in the same way you can end your conversations: Plead a prior commitment, thank the other person, summarize your agreement, show interest in future contact, or issue an invitation. Ending visits is perhaps most difficult when you are visiting someone more out of guilt than out of real interest, as is often the case when adult children visit their parents. There can be anxiety involved in leaving, even if the visit is no longer pleasant.

When you know in advance that you are going to meet with someone who you only want to see for a short while, notify the person in advance that your time is limited, "Yes, Mother, I'd love to come to dinner Thursday, but I have to leave no later than 7:30."

"I can drop in for 10 minutes on my way to the airport."

Then, when the time comes, you can be apologetic and very believable in pleading your prior commitment. "I'm glad you'd like me to stay longer, but I did tell you that I have other plans."

Suppose you want to end more than just a conversation or a visit — you want to end a relationship. That is the subject of the next chapter.

12

Ending Relationships

Many adult children want to end relationships but don't know how to go about it. If you find that a relationship that is unimportant to you is unsatisfying, a poor exchange, consider leaving it right away. Most times this can be accomplished simply by not calling, by not returning phone calls, and by answering invitations with, "Sorry, but I'm too busy."

If the relationship has been important to you, consider using the communication skills you learned earlier in this book. Many people find that active listening, asking for details, agreeing, the "When . . . then" formula, and other skills can enable them to turn their relationships around and once again feel good about them.

If using the communication skills in this book doesn't work, consider using the problem-solving formula in Chapter 6 to decide on the best course of action. If you do decide to end the relationship, it doesn't mean you don't care for the other person, though you may not. It means that you care for yourself more and that you have decided, for reasons that make sense to you, to go on without that person.

Even after you have made the decision, you may find yourself putting off ending the relationship because you don't want to hurt the other person. The result is that the other person is hurt more because he or she invests more — and you are hurt more because you are living a lie. Endings hurt. There is no way around it. There is loss for both even if you want out. To avoid reality is disrespectful of both the other person and yourself. The following suggestions should help make it easier for you to end relationships.

Practice beforehand. Rehearsing will enable you to plan exactly what you'll say, how you'll say it, and how you'll respond to likely comments from the other person. In addition, it will desensitize you to the situation.

Ask to meet in a public place. There is far less possibility of shouting or violence at a restaurant or a park than there is in the privacy of your home or apartment.

Meet in the morning. That will give the other person all day to think about the breakup and to call for support.

Be brief. The other person probably already knows what you have to say and will probably not be able to listen to much beyond your main statement anyway.

Stick to the present. Don't bring up old gripes, old grudges. Presenting your entire case against the other person may make you feel well justified in saying good-bye, but it is also highly likely to produce an argument. Do talk about the past — but do it later, with a friend.

Begin feelings messages with "I." Messages that begin with "I" describe your feelings without blaming the other person for them. For example: "I want to be independent." "I want to get to know myself." "I've changed, and I'm no longer happy being married." "I" messages are unlikely to move others to counterattack in order to defend themselves. Avoid messages beginning with "you"; they are often accusatory: "You are crude." "You are a lousy lover." "You made me miserable."

Announce your intentions. If you intend to seek a separation or divorce, or wish in some other way to end the relationship, make that clear. Many people are so vague in stating their intentions that the other person is left with only a cloudy idea that they are unhappy. If you have had children with the other person, let him know if you want and expect him to continue playing an active parenting role.

If you don't want to reconsider. Be very clear. Use active listening, agreeing, and broken record to show the other person he has been understood, and that you will no longer continue as before.

Second chances. If you have made your decision and it is irrevocable, stop reading here. On the other hand, if you're like many people, although your decision may be clear to you right now, you may have second thoughts later. Many adult children begin to doubt themselves after the initial relief of ending a troubled relationship passes. They have an energy letdown, and then the questioning begins: "Maybe he meant it this time." "Maybe she will change." "Maybe I made a mistake."

If you do decide to give the relationship a second chance, make specific demands. For example: (1) You will go into a rehabilitation center for treatment within ten days. (2) You will give me the promotion and the raise you promised by the end of the month. (3) We will go into counseling as a couple.

If the other person will not meet those demands, your decision will become even clearer. If they do agree, set up a time frame for action and agree to keep an open mind for a few months. If nothing changes in the additional time, follow through without further delay or discussion.

Endings allow for new beginnings. If you do not close the present, you cannot go on to the future. When relationships work, you can go on together. When they don't, endings open up room for new possibilities.

Getting Started

Knowing is not enough, we must apply.
Willing is not enough, we must do.

— Goethe

You now know the lifeskills, the tools, you never learned as a child. These skills can help you develop your potential. They can help you dramatically improve the quality of your life. But just *knowing* these skills isn't enough — it will take both knowing and *doing*.

At first you may not be very good at using these skills. Perhaps you'll be downright awkward. But that's how you and everyone else starts out with almost every skill we ever learn. Ever watch a baby learning the skills involved in walking? She sways too far to the left — and tumbles. She sways too far to the right — and tumbles. She steps too far forward — and tumbles. And with practice, she gets better and better at walking — and then pretty darn good. You were once a baby, and that's your story. All of us were once babies, and that's our story.

111

Many adult children think that if they aren't terrific at something immediately, they're no good and will never be any good. Don't you fall for that "black-or-white" type of thinking. Real life isn't like that. In real life, there's plenty of fumbling and tumbling in learning to walk, in learning any skill. And you never get perfect, but you can become pretty darn good. It takes effort and sometimes stubborn determination, but you did it with walking and talking and handwriting and hundreds of other skills, and you *can* do it with these lifeskills. So if you find some of these lifeskills difficult, be patient with yourself and stick with it, knowing you will improve with practice.

With these lifeskills, you can start becoming a more active participant in your life. With these lifeskills, you can improve the quality of your relationships. With these lifeskills, you can have more personal power. We wish you all these things, and we know that you will have them, if you will make the effort.

APPENDIX

A Program For Learning

Making contact with others, expressing feelings, active listening, asking for what you want, giving others what they want, ending conversations, and ending visits — these are skills you will be using almost every day. Instead of starting to practice all of them all at once, you may find it easier to get started gradually. Consider using the following program.

Increase Your Frequency

Pick one skill you would like to focus on first. If it is a skill you are already using, count how often you do so over the next two days. A good way of keeping track is to have a pen and paper in your purse or pocket and to make a note each time you use the skill. The average you arrive at over those two days will be your goal for the third day. Then, increase your goal by one each day until you arrive at a level you are happy with. For example, if you found that you asked no open questions the first day and two the second day, your goal for the third day would be one. The day after that, your goal would be two, and so forth, until you arrived at a level you were satisfied with, perhaps five or six. Write your goals down and put them on your bathroom mirror or in your datebook so you will take them seriously and will be frequently reminded of them.

If a skill you want to work on is new to you, set a goal of using it once the first day, twice the second day, and three times the third day, until you reach a level you'd like to maintain. Just as it is a lot easier to climb the fifth rung on a ladder after you have climbed the first four, by doing just a little more and then a little more than that, you can reach goals that may have seemed impossible at the beginning. As the saying goes, "Inch by inch, anything's a cinch!"

If you find one or more of the skills in this book particularly difficult for you, you may want to back up, add steps, and inch your way gradually to the point where you want to be. Suppose that the first skill you want to practice is starting conversations, and you are having difficulty doing so. You might find a point on the following list at which you would feel comfortable. Start there, and work your way from there.

- Smile at someone once a day for a week.
- Smile at two people a day for a week.
- Smile at three people a day for a week.
- Smile and say hello to someone once a day for a week.
- Smile and say hello to two people a day for a week.
- Smile and say hello to three people a day for a week.
- Smile, say hello, and ask someone you know a question about themselves or the situation once a day for a week.
- Smile, say hello, and ask two people you know a question about themselves or the situation twice a day for a week.

- Smile, say hello, and ask three people you know a question about themselves or the situation once a day for a week.
- Smile, say hello, and ask someone you do not know a question about themselves or the situation once a day for a week.
- Smile, say hello, and ask two people you do not know a question about themselves or the situation once a day for a week.
- Smile, say hello, and ask three people you do not know a question about themselves or the situation once a day for a week.

You can compose a similar list for any of the skills in this book. If you follow a list such as this, feel free to modify it according to your needs, for example by adding or skipping steps and by spending more or less time on steps. If you find yourself experiencing great anxiety at any point, you may want to seek professional help as you learn to use these skills.

When you arrive at a satisfactory frequency with your first skill, continue maintaining that level for the next week while you begin using the same procedure with another skill. Then keep track of your use of that first skill once every other day for the following week and then once a week for as long as you think worthwhile.

Reward Yourself

When you plan your goals, include a weekly — or even daily — reward that you will give yourself when you have done what you set out to do. Your reward might be a new shirt, a music tape, a drive in the city, or a nice warm bubble bath. Large or small, the only requirement is that your reward be something you want and would genuinely enjoy. When you reach your goal, be certain you immediately give yourself this reward. If you withhold it, you won't take yourself seriously when you promise yourself future rewards.

Compliment Yourself

Studies have shown that assertive people often compliment themselves for speaking up. Even when they don't get what they want, they typically compliment themselves for having made the effort. With that in mind, compliment yourself frequently as you work on your goals:

"I did it!"

"I'm really making progress!"

As usual, specific compliments are best: "Congratulations! You had good eye contact, a steady hand, and asked a good open question."

Consider your goals achieved when you do what you set out to do, regardless of how others respond. Most times the response will be positive; other times it won't. Even when it isn't, when you use these skills, you are on the road to success, so praise yourself: "I'm proud of you for telling Larry you really like him. I know that wasn't easy, but *you did it!* Even though he just smiled and said he had to be going, I bet he was really pleased."

Rehearse

You will find it helpful to rehearse each day using the skills you are working on, both with friends and in your mind. Just as rehearsals prepare actors to do better, so they can help you be far more at ease and far more skillful. Tell those you rehearse with always to respond positively. Your practice sessions with others and in your mind are the best of all worlds — you always get a yes, you always win. When you make a mistake, don't put yourself down and "awfulize" about it. Instead, simply go back and practice some more. When you rehearse in your mind, picture the scene as clearly and as vividly as you can. *Be* the person using the skill, rather than someone watching it on television. *Smell* the odors, *hear* the sounds, *see* the people, just as vividly as you can. Basketball, football, hockey players, public speakers — successful people from all walks of life can attest to the tremendous value of imagining success over and over in your mind before you go for the real thing. What you see in your mind can be what you get.

Solving problems, asking others to change their behavior, handling criticism, establishing and defending boundaries, fighting fair, and ending relationships are skills you won't be able to set frequency goals for as you will use them only once in a while. You will, however, be able to set goals for using them in given situations. "The next time I see Pat, I'm going to ask him please not to call after ten except in an emergency." "The next time my mother criticizes me for seeing Roger, I'm going to agree with the truth, agree with the odds, and agree with the critic's right to differ." As with the daily goals, write these goals down, rehearse using them with others and in your mind, and reward and compliment yourself.

About The Authors

Janet Geringer Woititz, Ed.D., is the founder and President of the Institute for Counseling and Training in West Caldwell, New Jersey, which specializes in working with dysfunctional families and individuals. She is the author of the best-selling *Adult Children Of Alcoholics* and *Struggle For Intimacy* as well as *Marriage On The Rocks, Healing Your Sexual Self* and *The Self-Sabotage Syndrome: Adult Children In The Workplace*. Her books are also available as tapes.

Alan Garner, M.A., is a nationally known relationship-skills trainer who lives in Laguna Hills, California. He is the author of *A Search For Meaning, Conversationally Speaking,* and the million-selling parent/child manual *It's OK to Say No to Drugs!*